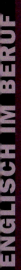
ENGLISCH IM BERUF

English for Logistics

Marion Grussendorf

SHORT COURSE
SERIES

Verfasser	Marion Grussendorf
Originalausgabe	erschienen bei Oxford University Press
Originaltitel	Express Series – English for Logistics, Copyright © 2009
Verlagsredaktion	Gary Helft, Murdo MacPhail
Redaktionelle Mitarbeit	Oliver Busch (Wortliste), Rani Kumar
Bildredaktion	Nicole Simone Abt
Gesamtgestaltung	Sylvia Lang
Layout und technische Umsetzung	Andrea Päch, Berlin
Quellen	*Titelfoto:* © iStockphoto, Steve Cole
	Symbole und Illustrationen: Andreas Terglane, Kassel
	Fotos: **5** iStockphoto/R Sherwood Veith | **6** iStockphoto/Dan Driedger | **7.1** iStockphoto/Silvrshootr | **7.2** Bananastock (RF) | **7.3** iStockphoto/Steve Cole | **10** Fotolia/Flying-Tiger | **11** iStockphoto/David Pedre | **12** Fotolia/Eisenhans | **15** iStockphoto/Jonathan Heger | **19** iStockphoto/clu | **23** iStockphoto/Michael DeLeon | **25** iStockphoto/Tor Lindqvist | **27** iStockphoto/Pali Rao | **28.1** Wikimedia Commons, GNU/Marcus Wong | **28.2** iStockphoto/Olivier Lantzendörffer | **28.3** Wikipedia/GFDL/Bryan Flint | **28.4** iStockphoto/Maciej Noskowski | **28.5** iStockphoto/Adrian Assalve | **28.6** Wikipedia/gemeinfrei | **29** iStockphoto/Rudyanto Wijaya | **31.1** Wikipedia/GFDL | **31.2** iStockphoto/Joerg Reimann | **31.3** Fotolia/Sapsiwai | **31.4** iStockphoto/ictor | **33.1** Wikipedia/gemeinfrei | **33.2** Wikipedia/GFDL | **33.3** iStockphoto/Kirsty Pargeter | **34.2** shutterstock/Frank Boston | **35** shutterstock/Anyka | **36** Wikipedia, GFDL | **37.1** iStockphoto/Tor Lindqvist | **37.2** Wikipedia/gemeinfrei | **44** iStockphoto/William Voon | **50.1** iStockphoto/oonal | **50.2** iStockphoto/Yuriy Chaban | **50.3** iStockphoto/David Cannings-Bushell | **50.4** iStockphoto/Jorgen Jacobsen | **50.5** iStockphoto/Angelilka Stern | **52** Wikimedia Commons/gemeinfrei | **53.1** iStockphoto/Jorgen Jacobsen | **53.2** Fotolia/mipan | **53.3** kind permission Roll Containers Handling Ltd | **53.4** Fotolia/fefufotol **53.5** Fotolia/Julián Rovagnati | **53.6** Fotolia/Alexey | **57** iStockphoto/endopack | **58** iStockphoto/ugur bariskan | **59** iStockphoto/Ulrich Koch | **60** iStockphoto/RonTech2000 | **65** Fotolia/Anne Katrin Figge | **69** iStockphoto/Christine Glade | **72** shutterstock/Frank Boston | **73** Wikipedia/gemeinfrei

The authors and publisher are grateful to those who have given permission to reproduce the following extracts and adaptations of copyright material: p15 www.jobfunctions.bnet.com; p23 www.careerjet.hk

Weitere Titel in der *Short Course Series*:	
English for Accounting	ISBN 978-3-464-20480-1
English for the Automobile Industry	ISBN 978-3-464-20479-5
English for Customer Care	ISBN 978-3-464-01882-8
English for Emails	ISBN 978-3-464-20007-0
English for the Energy Industry	ISBN 978-3-464-20385-9
English for Human Resources	ISBN 978-3-464-20481-8
English for Legal Professionals	ISBN 978-3-464-20386-6
English for Marketing and Advertising	ISBN 978-3-464-01876-7
English for Meetings	ISBN 978-3-464-01874-3
English for Negotiating	ISBN 978-3-464-20224-1
English for the Pharmaceutical Industry	ISBN 978-3-464-20387-3
English for Presentations	ISBN 978-3-464-01875-0
English for Real Estate	ISBN 978-3-464-20006-3
English for Sales and Purchasing	ISBN 978-3-464-20225-8
English for Socializing and Small Talk	ISBN 978-3-464-20156-5
English for Telephoning	ISBN 978-3-464-01873-6

www.cornelsen.de

Die Links zu externen Webseiten Dritter, die in diesem Lehrwerk angegeben sind, wurden vor Drucklegung sorgfältig auf ihre Aktualität geprüft. Der Verlag übernimmt keine Gewähr für die Aktualität und den Inhalt dieser Seiten oder solcher, die mit ihnen verlinkt sind.

1. Auflage, 1. Druck 2010

Alle Drucke dieser Auflage sind inhaltlich unverändert und können im Unterricht nebeneinander verwendet werden.

© 2010 Cornelsen Verlag, Berlin

Das Werk und seine Teile sind urheberrechtlich geschützt. Jede Nutzung in anderen als den gesetzlich zugelassenen Fällen bedarf der vorherigen schriftlichen Einwilligung des Verlages.
Hinweis zu den §§ 46, 52 a UrhG: Weder das Werk noch seine Teile dürfen ohne eine solche Einwilligung eingescannt und in ein Netzwerk eingestellt oder sonst öffentlich zugänglich gemacht werden. Dies gilt auch für Intranets von Schulen und sonstigen Bildungseinrichtungen.

Druck: CS-Druck CornelsenStürtz, Berlin

ISBN 978-3-464-20194-7

 Inhalt gedruckt auf säurefreiem Papier aus nachhaltiger Forstwirtschaft.

Contents

PAGE	UNIT TITLE	TOPICS	USEFUL LANGUAGE AND STRUCTURES
5	**1 Introduction to logistics**	Setting the scene Jobs in logistics Regular activities	Describing jobs Talking about regular activities
12	**2 Logistics services**	Logistics acronyms Product ranges 3PL providers Valuse-added services	Selling services Explaining online services
20	**3 Inventory management and procurement**	Inventory management Continuous replenishment Job advertisements	The passive Giving and asking for opinions Making suggestions Agreeing
28	**4 Modes of transport**	Transport and handling equipment Container types Types of goods	Adjectives Making comparisons Describing features
37	**5 Planning and arranging transport**	Transport options Measurements Quotations	Making enquiries and requests Advising and offering alternatives Numbers, dimensions, and weight
45	**6 Shipping goods**	Markings Loading Advice of shipment Shipping instructions	Explainings how to do something Prepositions Talking about shipping problems
53	**7 Warehousing and storage**	Handling equipment Warehouse areas Warehousing today	The passive with modals Talking about improvements Describing a process
60	**8 Documentation and finance**	Documents in foreign trade Import instructions Payment methods	Apologizing *by* and *until* Handling payments Dealing with mistakes

PAGE	APPENDIX
70	**Test yourself!**
72	**Partner files Partner A**
73	**Partner files Partner B**
74	**Answer key**
82	**Transcripts**
87	**A–Z word lists**
93	**Useful phrases**
95	**Glossary of acronyms and abbreviations**
96	**Weights and measures conversion chart**

Vorwort

Durch die zunehmende Internationalisierung der Bereiche Logistik und Transport ist für viele Mitarbeiter in der Logistikbranche die Notwendigkeit gewachsen, mit Kunden, Lieferanten oder Geschäftspartnern auf Englisch zu kommunizieren. Mit **English for Logistics** erlernen Sie gezielt die Fachbegriffe, Redewendungen und Vokabeln, die Sie brauchen, um typische Situationen im Berufsalltag zu bewältigen.

In **English for Logistics** finden Sie eine Reihe von Themen, die für eine berufliche Tätigkeit in der Logistik von Bedeutung sind. Diese umfassen z. B. verschiedene Logistikdienstleistungen, Lagerverwaltungssysteme, Transportarten, Transportplanung, Versand und wichtige Dokumente im internationalen Handel. Neben der Einführung wichtiger Fachterminologie steht dabei die sprachliche Umsetzung von Aufgaben, die Mitarbeiter in der Logistik meistern müssen, im Vordergrund. Die Übungsaufgaben decken die folgenden Bereiche ab: Kundenberatung und -information, Einholung und Abgabe von Angeboten, Erteilung von Anweisungen, Besprechen und Lösen von Problemen, Beschreibung von Abläufen, korrekte Verwendung von Maßeinheiten, Klärung von Zahlungsmodalitäten und vieles mehr.

English for Logistics umfasst acht Units, die die wichtigsten Themenfelder abdecken. Jede Unit beginnt mit einer kurzen Übung **Upload**, einer Aufwärmübung, die auf das jeweilige Thema einstimmt. Im Folgenden bereitet jede Unit einen realistischen Arbeitskontext auf, in dem das neue Fachwissen und die dazugehörigen sprachlichen Mittel vermittelt werden. Zahlreiche Übungen und Hörtexte auf der beiliegenden CD helfen das Erlernte im Kontext anzuwenden. So können Sie Ihr Wissen überprüfen, neue Fachbegriffe und Redewendungen lernen oder bestimmte Strukturen üben. Zu vielen Aufgaben gibt es einen **Vocabulary Assistant**, der wichtige Wörter und Redewendungen übersetzt. **Useful Phrases**-Kästen enthalten gängige Redewendungen aus dem jeweiligen Themenfeld. **Did you know?** liefert zusätzliche Erklärungen von Begriffen, die im Logistikkontext wichtig sind.

Jede Unit schließt mit dem Abschnitt **Offload** ab, der einen authentischen Text aus der Fachpresse präsentiert, zur persönlichen Stellungnahme einlädt und zur weiteren Diskussion anregt.

In den Units finden Sie Übungen mit Verweisen auf die **Partner files** im Anhang. Diese zusätzlichen Partner-Übungen helfen Ihnen, den in der Unit erlernten Wortschatz in typischen Situationen zu trainieren.

Der Band schließt mit einem Kreuzworträtsel, bei dem der neue Wortschatz angewendet werden kann: **Test yourself!**

Im Anhang von **English for Logistics** finden Sie den **Answer key**, mit dem Sie Ihre Antworten selbstständig überprüfen können. Der Anhang enthält außerdem die **Partner files** sowie eine **A–Z word list**. Unter **Useful phrases and vocabulary** können Sie nützliche Redewendungen und Begriffe nachschlagen, die Sie für bestimmte Tätigkeiten in der Logistik benötigen.

Viel Spaß und viel Erfolg wünschen Ihnen Autorin und Redaktion!

1 Introduction to logistics

Upload

Make a list of the different areas of logistics you can think of. Complete the diagram below.

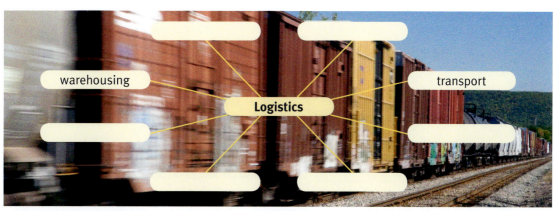

- warehousing
- transport
- Logistics

1 Five people give a definition of logistics. Complete the sentences using the words from the box.

provide • storage • support • distribution • delivery • maintenance

1. *Logistics* means that you manage the procurement and movement of goods and the _____ of inventory.

2. It means the _____ of the goods the customer needs at the right time, in the right place, and of the right quality.

3. My definition of *logistics* is this: it's to plan, organize, and manage operations that _____ services and goods.

4. *Logistics* – that's the purchasing, maintenance, _____, and replacement of material and staff.

5. *Logistics* is the planning and _____ of operations such as warehousing, inventory, transport, procurement, supply, and _____.

Listen to the recording and check your answers.

Vocabulary Assistant **V**
procurement *Beschaffung*
maintenance *Wartung, Instandhaltung*
distribution *Vertrieb, Auslieferung*   purchasing *Einkauf*

2 Complete the following table using the words from exercise 1.

	Verb	Noun
1	to provide	
2		storage
3	to support	
4		delivery
5		distribution
6	to maintain	
7		transportation
8		purchasing

3 Now complete the sentences with the correct form of the words from the table.

1 In my job I oversee the _____ of vehicles and machinery.
2 Do they also _____ parcels and packages on Sundays?
3 Goods are normally bought in the _____ department.
4 We _____ a 24-hour delivery service.
5 This company only _____ goods by road.
6 We _____ all our goods in the warehouse.

4 Match the definitions (a–f) with the words (1–6) below.

1 carrier ☐
2 freight forwarder ☐
3 supplier ☐
4 haulage contractor/haulier ☐
5 courier ☐
6 consignee ☐

a company which carries goods by road
b person or firm named in a freight contract to whom goods have been shipped or turned over for care
c company that specializes in the speedy and secure delivery of small goods and packages
d company that transports or conveys goods
e company which supplies parts or services to another company; also called vendor
f person or business that arranges documentation and travel facilities for companies dispatching goods to customers

UNIT **1** Introduction to logistics | **7**

5 **Listen to three people describing their jobs in logistics: a warehouse manager, a freight forwarder, and a shipping operations manager. Match each job to the correct person.**

1 _____   2 _____   3 _____

> **Vocabulary Assistant**
>
> to consolidate *zusammenstellen*
> customs clearance *Zollabfertigung*
> quotation *Angebot, Kostenvoranschlag*
> sophisticated *hochentwickelt*   to retrieve *wiederfinden*
> to liaise with *zusammenarbeiten mit*   on behalf of *im Auftrag von*

6 **Now listen again and complete the sentences.**

Person 1

1 My job is to _____ the transport of goods either by sea, air, road, or rail.

2 An important part of the job is _____ with customer requests about the most suitable mode of transport.

3 My responsibilities also include _____ good shipping rates with shipping lines and transport companies.

4 I _____ customs clearance on behalf of my clients.

Person 2

5 In my job I have to _____ that the cargo is not damaged onboard the ship or while loading or unloading.

6 I _____ customers on shipping rates and prepare quotations for our sales office.

Person 3

7 Another part of my job is to _____ with departments such as transport and production.

8 Apart from that, I _____ that vehicles, machines, and any other kind of equipment are maintained to a high level.

7 Match the verbs (1–8) with the activities (a–h) to make phrases from the recordings. Then listen again to check if necessary.

1 book
2 consolidate
3 deal
4 keep
5 make
6 use
7 check
8 take care

a a number of shipments under one bill of lading
b booking reservations
c that health and safety standards are maintained
d modern computer systems
e space on a ship, train, lorry, or plane
f where to put them in the warehouse
g an eye on the budget
h with all the necessary documentation

8 Work with a partner to describe two different jobs. The phrases in the box will help you.

TALKING ABOUT JOB RESPONSIBILITIES *Useful phrases*

Questions
What do you do?
What's your line of work?
What does your job involve?

Describing jobs
I work for a major shipping company.
I work in the regional depot.

Describing responsibilities
I'm responsible for …
In my job I have to …
My job involves …

Remember …
You work **for** or **at** a company.
You work **in** an area or a department.
You are responsible **for** or in charge **of** something.

Here are some useful verbs for describing key job responsibilities:

to advise
to prepare
to train
to manage
to estimate
to monitor
to carry out

to oversee
to provide or supply
to ensure
to review
to liaise with
to organize

Vocabulary Assistant
to carry out *ausführen*
to estimate *schätzen, abschätzen*
to oversee *beaufsichtigen, überwachen*

PARTNER FILES
Partner A File 01, p. 72
Partner B File 09, p. 73

DELIVERY • DISPATCH • SHIPMENT • SUPPLY *Did you know*

Delivery (to deliver) is to **take** letters or products to the places to where they are addressed.
Delivery is the taking of letters, products etc. to somebody or somewhere.
Who is responsible for delivery? (for taking the products from A to B)

Dispatch (to dispatch) – the activity of **sending** products. The consignment is first dispatched by the sender and when it arrives at the destination, it has been delivered
When was the consignment dispatched? (when was it sent from the supplier)

Shipment (to ship): the process of transporting products especially by ship. However it can be used in relation to other methods when specified e.g. we will arrange shipment by air.
Can you arrange shipment in the next few days? (the transportation)

Supply (to supply): to provide a company or person with products or services.
Our company supplies computer chips to Intel. (we provide the product

UNIT **1** Introduction to logistics | **9**

9 Replace the underlined verbs with words from the box that have the same meaning.

provide • train • organize • ensure • inform about • check

1 We <u>supply</u> software for the car industry. _____

2 I often <u>advise</u> clients <u>on</u> the most suitable transport method. _____

3 In my job I have to <u>make sure</u> that passengers arrive on schedule. _____

4 My job is to <u>supervise</u> incoming goods. _____

5 I also <u>plan</u> the transport of goods. _____

6 I <u>instruct</u> staff. _____

10 Complete the form with your own job details. Use complete sentences and expressions from this unit.

Job profile: _____
Company: *I work for* _____
Job title: _____
Main responsibilities: _____
_____
_____
3 – 5 key activities: _____
_____
_____
_____
_____

TALKING ABOUT REGULAR ACTIVITIES — Did you know?

When talking about general facts and describing what we normally do, we use the present simple. It is often used with words that say how often something happens, e.g. *usually, often, always, sometimes, every,* etc. We use the verb *do* to make questions and negative statements:
  I work for *an international logistics company.*
  He **usually spends** *a lot of time with his customers.*
  Do *you* **ship** *goods to Asia?*
  He **doesn't work** *in the European office.*

11 Put the words in the right order. Use the correct form of the verb.

1. an excellent / provide / delivery service / my company.
2. you / how much / handle / cargo / per year ?
3. to other countries / not ship / we / chemical products.
4. responsible for / be / the warehouse manager / also / vehicles and machinery.
5. to foreign companies / car parts / this vendor / supply ?
6. usually / arrange / for companies / a freight forwarder / documentation.

12 Work with a partner. Follow the steps below to practise this dialogue.

A Ask B what he/she does.
B Respond. Tell A where you work.
A Ask B to give you some details about the job.
B Tell A about your main job activities. Then ask A about his/her job.
A Respond. Describe your job activities.

13 Complete the crossword puzzle with words from this unit.

Across
4 Another word for freight.
5 What you store in the warehouse.
6 Work closely together with somebody.

Down
1 Another word for organize.
2 To give information about the price.
3 Another word for supervise.
5 Send goods.

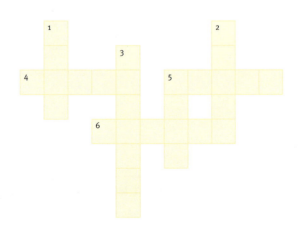

14 Translate the following sentences.

1. Ich arbeite bei einer großen internationalen Spedition.
2. Wir haben ein großes Vertriebsnetzwerk in Europa.
3. Was machen Sie beruflich?
4. Er arbeitet im Einkauf.
5. Ich kümmere mich im Auftrag meiner Kunden um die Zollabfertigung.

Read the article and answer the questions.

CHINA'S BOOMING EXPORT BUSINESS

China's economy is developing at a rapid pace with double-digit growth rates in export business and an expected increase of 40 per cent by 2010. With an estimated trade volume of nearly 2 trillion US dollars in 2006, China handles more cargo than any other country in the world. Given these growth rates, it is not surprising that the Chinese logistics sector increased by more than 12 per cent last year.

In order to support the booming industry, the government is currently investing massively in the country's infrastructure. Over the next few years, the Chinese government wants to improve and extend the existing road and railway networks as well as maritime harbours and airports.

For transport logistics, Shanghai is one of the most attractive locations in China. It is the second largest city in the country and has good links to the most important industrial regions. And Shanghai is also a modern and welcoming host for visitors and business people from China and around the world.

Vocabulary Assistant
double-digit *zweistellig*   host *Gastgeber/in, Veranstalter/in*
link *Verbindung*   trade volume *Handelsvolumen*

Over to you

- Do you know any other countries with considerable export growth rates?
- How does logistics play an important role in a country's economy?
- What do you know about the logistics industry in your country?

2 Logistics services

Logistics uses many acronyms. How many do you know? Test yourself by writing these ones out.

1. FCL _____
2. 3PL _____
3. HGV _____
4. DC _____
5. LCL _____
6. EDI _____
7. VAS _____
8. RFID _____
9. ISO _____
10. GPS _____

1 Match the words (1–8) with their definitions (a–h) below.

1. transshipment ☐
2. break-bulk ☐
3. cross-docking ☐
4. order picking ☐
5. reverse logistics ☐
6. tracking and tracing ☐
7. warehousing ☐
8. collection ☐

a direct flow of goods from receipt at warehouse to shipping, bypassing storage
b collecting and handling of used or damaged goods or of reusable transit equipment
c loading goods from one means of carriage onto another
d selecting and assembling items from stock for shipments
e packing goods in small, separable units
f picking up goods at a named place
g receiving and storing goods
h locating items in transit

2 Look at these words from exercise 1 and use your dictionary (if necessary) to complete the table.

	Verb	Noun
1	receive	
2		equipment
3	carry	
4		assembly
5		location

3 Listen to three logistics providers presenting their services. Complete the table.

> **Vocabulary Assistant**
> competitive *günstig* consignment *Warensendung, Lieferung* customized *maßgeschneidert* to meet requirements *Anforderungen erfüllen*

	specializes in	transport mode used
Provider 1 (GFT Global Carrier)		
Provider 2 (Home Tex International)		
Provider 3 (Cargo Express)		

4 Listen to the recording again and complete the sentences.

> provider • shipping lines • fleet of vehicles • air carriers • transport companies • documentation

1. We are one of the world's leading _____ with a freight volume of 600,000 containers per year.
2. We can offer our customers competitive rates with all major _____.
3. With a modern _____, we can ensure fast, safe delivery of your consignments.
4. Our services include order picking, packing, distribution, and handling of all transport _____.
5. Cargo Express is Asia's leading _____ of air freight services.
6. We work closely with _____ around the world for the fastest delivery available.

5 Complete the sentences with words from the box.

> happy • provide • range • specialize • major • ensure • customized

1 As a _____ non-vessel operating common carrier, we can offer our customers competitive rates with all major shipping lines.

2 We _____ in solutions for full container loads (FCL) and less than container consolidated loads (LCL).

3 As a specialist in home textiles, we can offer our clients _____ services to meet their needs.

4 Our team will be _____ to assist you in all matters regarding your order.

5 We can _____ you with tailor-made solutions for your air transport requirements.

6 We closely co-operate with air carriers around the world and can offer our customers a wide _____ of flexible and cost-effective services.

Now listen and check your answers.

SELLING YOUR COMPANY'S LOGISTICS SERVICES TO THE CUSTOMER

Useful phrases

When describing a company's services or portfolio, we often use the following expressions:
We can offer you a wide range of ...
We can provide (you with) customized/tailor-made logistics solutions for ...
We specialize in ...
As a specialist for/in ... we can ...
With our many years of experience ...
We have experience and expertise in providing ...
Our team will be happy to handle/assist you ...
With our dedicated team of logistics experts we can ...

---

6 Complete the list with your own company's services. Then present it to your partner using phrases from this unit.

1 range of products or services   _____

2 specialist in   _____

3 experience   _____

4 extra services for customers   _____

7 Present the company's services to your partner. Use phrases from this unit.

PARTNER FILES Partner A File 02, p. 72
Partner B File 10, p. 73

8 Read the following text from a logistics company magazine about new trends in third-party logistics. Then label the paragraphs with the correct headings from the list.

Today's role of major providers • Changing logistics requirements for manufacturers • 3PL in the past • New challenges for 3PL • Change in logistics concepts

Recent trends in 3PL

1 _____

Until a few years ago, companies used to outsource only parts of their logistics operations to providers specializing in services such as distribution or warehousing. A single company sometimes had several third-party logistics providers (3PLs).

2 _____

The globalization of trade and increasing demand for services, however, has led to a drastic shift in logistics concepts and management with an impact on both producers and logistics providers.

3 _____

As far as manufacturers are concerned, logistics management has become a lot more complex. By now, many of them have learned that outsourcing single segments to different providers has not really made their logistics operations more efficient. That is why they are looking for providers who can provide a higher level of service and more comprehensive supply chain solutions.

4 _____

For 3PLs all over the world, requirements keep getting more demanding with customers asking for a wider range of logistics solutions. Apart from that, logistics providers today are facing an increasingly tough and highly competitive market. In recent years, growing pressure on prices has led to a decrease in profit margins. In order to compensate for this, many third-party logistics providers now offer value-added services for their customers. Due to fierce competition in the 3PL market, however, experts predict that only the big international players will be able to work profitably in the future.

5 _____

The big global players, also called super-3PLs, can provide their customers with comprehensive supply chain or end-to-end solutions. These services usually include forwarding, transportation, consolidation, customs brokerage, warehousing, and distribution, as well as a range of value-added services.

9 Now say which of these statements are true (T) or false (F).

1. In the past, companies used to outsource only segments of their logistics operations.
2. Manufacturers found out that outsourcing to 3PL providers is not efficient.
3. In the past few years many 3PL providers have increased their profit margins.
4. Customers today are demanding more complex logistics solutions.
5. Super-3PLs provide comprehensive solutions to logistics problems.

10 Match the words (1–6) from the text with the correct definition (a–f).

1. outsourcing
2. comprehensive
3. consolidation
4. requirements
5. demand
6. competition

a including a wide range of services
b details of what is expected and needed
c contracting functions out to third-party providers
d the need for particular goods or services
e companies trying to sell the same or similar products to customers
f the grouping of small shipments into one container

11 Look at the three website advertisements for value-added services. Then complete the table.

Maxwell Express Logistics

Warehousing is just one of the integrated logistics services we provide. Here are some value-added services we can offer:

- Pick and pack
- Literature fulfilment
- Returns processing
- Credit processing
- … and much more!

Sichuan International Logistics

Our logistics team at Sichuan International Logistics has the experience and expertise to provide our customers with value-added services that complement their basic warehouse operations. Our services include:

- Kitting
- Import/export cargo customs clearance
- Packaging services
- Export packing and crating

UNIT **2** Logistics services | **17**

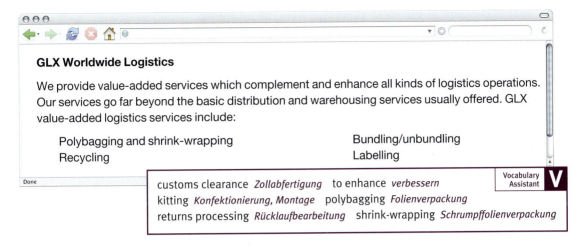

	payment	documentation	product assembly	packing / packaging	other services
Maxwell Express Logistics					
Sichuan International Logistics					
GLX Worldwide Logistics					

12 **Listen to two short presentations about online logistics services. Then say which of the statements are true (T) or false (F).**

Express Logistics Online Shipping

1 ... helps you book pick-ups and track shipments. ☐
2 ... you can log on by selecting your country. ☐
3 ... you can check shipment records for up to 60 days. ☐

Intercargo E-Shipping

4 ... allows you to make price enquiries. ☐
5 ... you can cancel orders. ☐
6 ... you can download pdf documents. ☐

> **Vocabulary Assistant**
> collection *Abholung*
> enquiry *Anfrage*
> to keep track of sth *etw (eine Sendung) verfolgen*
> request *Wunsch, Bitte, Anfrage*

> **Useful phrases**
> **EXPLAINING ONLINE SERVICES**
> When describing online functions or tools, you can use the following phrases and expressions:
>
> The price request tool allows you to obtain prices for shipments.
> E-Shipping helps you prepare/print/track/select ... online.
> To ... , (just) sign up/register for/log on to ...
> For price requests, please use ...
> To access shipment details, click ...

13 Match 1–6 with a–f to make sentences from the recording.

1. With Quick Online Shipping you can find
2. This online tool allows you
3. To use QOS, simply log on
4. After registering with E-Shipping, you can make
5. You can also
6. With a mouse click you can also

a to plan shipments, book collections and deliveries.
b price requests, schedule transport, and obtain real-time shipment information.
c track pick-ups and deliveries.
d download commercial documents in pdf format.
e by selecting your town or region from the drop-down menu on the left.
f the right service to suit your shipping needs.

14 IT has changed many people's jobs. Complete the statements with words from the box.

RFID • enter • track • mobile phone • device • digital • GPS-based • tag

Customer
Tracking shipments is a lot easier with SMS-Fast Track. Now I can use my _____ ¹ to find out where my shipment is. I just have to _____ ² my air waybill number on my mobile and wait a few seconds. Then I get a reply with the details of my consignment's current status. It's such a great idea!

Manager at a trailer storage yard
I work at a trailer yard where trailers filled with packaged goods are kept until they go out to the customers. The site is very large and we have four different areas for trailer storage. Until the new _____ ³ tag system was introduced, it could easily take a couple of hours to find the trailer we wanted. Now it's a matter of minutes to locate the vehicle we're looking for. All we have to do now is put the _____ ⁴ on a trailer and use a mobile _____ ⁵ to identify it. It really saves us a lot of time.

Truck driver
All our trucks are equipped with a _____ ⁶ truck support system now. For me that's a great help as I can always use maps that show me exactly where I am and where I have to go. Obviously, it's also useful for the company. They can _____ ⁷ my vehicle at any time, see the route I'm taking and where I make stops. And what's very handy for me – the system also comes with a _____ ⁸ camera so I can take photos if there's a problem while I'm on the road.

15 Translate the following sentences.

1. Wir bieten maßgeschneiderte Lösungen für Ihr Transportgeschäft.
2. Mit einem Mausklick können Sie Dokumente im PDF-Format herunterladen.
3. Unser Team wird Ihnen gerne bei Fragen behilflich sein.
4. Es erlaubt Ihnen, Lieferungen zu planen und Ihre Warensendungen zu verfolgen.
5. Um Preisanfragen zu machen, loggen Sie sich zunächst auf unserer Webseite ein.

Offload

Read the article and answer the questions.

A new tracking device for US postal services

An American company based in California has recently developed a tracking device which may help post offices to improve their services. It can be used to find out more about hold-ups and delays in postal operations.

The small tracker, called the Letter Logger, uses the Global Positioning System (GPS) to store information about an item's position in transit. Similar devices have been used in the past to track expensive consumer goods like cars, but until now none of these systems was small enough to travel in an envelope.

Now that's all changed. As well as fitting into a US standard-size business letter, the GPS Letter Logger also meets other postal requirements: it is bendable and able to withstand rough handling. This is particularly important as the envelopes are thrown into sacks, then transported by van to automatic sorting locations where they run through high-speed shuffling systems.

The tracker itself does not transmit its position during transit, but stores the journey log on a memory card which can be read by a laptop computer. The GPS device offers several programming options ranging from checking its position every few minutes to checking only when on the move.

The Letter Logger does not help, however, if the envelope carrying it does not arrive at its destination within about seven days, as the battery runs flat after about a week. ■

> **Vocabulary Assistant**
>
> bendable *biegsam*   device *Gerät*
> (to) fit into *hinein passen*   hold-up *Verzögerung*
> in transit *unterwegs, während des Transports*   run flat *leer werden*
> shuffling system *Sortiersystem*   (to) withstand *aushalten*

Over to you

- Have you ever experienced delays in postal services when sending or receiving letters?
- Do you think this device should be used in your home country's postal service?
- Do you know any other useful electronic devices in logistics and transport?

3 Inventory management and procurement

Check your knowledge of key terms in inventory management and procurement by choosing the best definitions for these terms.

1 **Economies of scale:**
   a Reducing costs per unit by increasing production
   b Cutting costs by reducing output

2 **Buffer stock:**
   a Goods kept in store to cover seasonal demand e. g. Christmas sale
   b Goods kept in store to cover unforeseen shortages or fluctuations in demand

3 **Factory gate pricing:**
   a Transport costs are not included in the purchase price of a product
   b The price is lower because you buy directly from the manufacturer

4 **Supply chain:**
   a The close co-operation of all parties involved in the making, selling, and delivering of a product
   b Network of stores that supply customers with a wide variety of products

5 **Tender:**
   a An assessment or calculation of the approximate cost or value of a product or service
   b An offer for goods or services that follows a request for a quotation made by an official body, e.g. local government

1 Match the beginnings of the sentences (1–6) with the endings (a–f) to make definitions of more key terms.

1 Lead time is the time
2 Procurement is
3 A retailer is a business
4 Customer order cycle time is the time
5 A wholesaler is
6 JIT – just in time is a concept

a customers are prepared to wait for the delivery of their order.
b of reducing inventories by co-ordinating the delivery of materials just before they are needed.
c it takes to produce and supply a product.
d an intermediary between manufacturers and retailers which buys in large quantities and resells in smaller quantities.
e that buys products from wholesalers or manufacturers and resells them to the ultimate consumer.
f the purchasing of goods (materials, parts, supplies, equipment) required to run an enterprise.

UNIT **3** Inventory management and procurement | **21**

2 **Listen to an expert presenting an inventory management system to the managers of a large retail store. Then say which of the statements are true (T) or false (F).**

1. The inventory system is called CPR.
2. It's a sales-based system.
3. The system co-ordinates the flow of information and goods in the logistic chain.
4. Young Fashion has used the system for six years now.
5. Orders are electronically transferred to the warehouse.
6. The store has reduced transport and inventory costs by about 25 per cent.

3 **Listen again and complete the sentences with the words from the box.**

> stock • lead times • replenishment • processing • generated • data interchange • point • schedule • inventory • retailer

1. Today I'm going to tell you something about CRP, that means continuous _____.
2. I'll also explain how it can be used to lower inventory and operational costs and to shorten product _____.
3. First of all, you decide what products you want to order at what _____ level.
4. The system will use this information at the _____ of sale in the retail store.
5. The leading Russian clothes _____ Young Fashion introduced continuous replenishment three years ago.
6. With the new system all orders are _____ by computers, which process data received from cash registers.
7. The orders are sent to the warehouse by electronic _____, where they are processed.
8. And finally the goods are delivered to the different outlets according to a _____.
9. Since the introduction of the CRP system, Young Fashion have managed to cut _____ and transport costs by about 15 %.
10. Moreover, errors in order _____ have been reduced considerably by using scanning technology and EDI.

Vocabulary Assistant

cash register *Kasse*
electronic data interchange *elektronischer Datenaustausch*
to generate *erzeugen, generieren, erwirtschaften* lead time *Durchlaufzeit, Vorlaufzeit* replenishment *Bestandauffüllung* retailer *Einzelhändler*

THE PASSIVE

Useful phrases

We often use the passive voice to describe processes, especially if we are more interested in the action itself than in the person who does the action. It is formed using the verb to be and the past participle (third form of the verb). We use by at the end of the sentence to say who or what does the action.

The goods **are delivered** to a depot.
The order **is generated** by the computer.

4 Put the processes described in the presentation about CRP in the correct order.

1 _____
2 _____
3 _____
4 _____
5 _____
6 _____

(Retail outlet, Computer system, Warehouse)

a Orders are generated based on data received from cash register.
b Goods are delivered to the retail outlet.
c System is activated at the point of sale.
d Orders are sent to the warehouse.
e Orders are processed.
f Sales information is transferred to the CRP computer system.

5 Here are some more inventory management techniques. Complete the sentences with the passive form of the verbs in brackets.

1 A system in which the inventory _____ (monitor), planned and managed by the manufacturer on behalf of the customer (often a retailer).

2 A system which is similar to CRP. It _____ (use, often) for products that need to be supplied frequently and in small batch sizes.

3 It means that orders _____ (transfer) electronically to the manufacturer. Then they _____ (deliver) to the retail store.

4 Real-time demand _____ (identify) by electronic cash register and the product movement _____ (co-ordinate) from supplier to the retail store.

5 Products that have similar characteristics regarding their selling profile _____ (categorize) into 'families'.

6 Now match the planning techniques below with the definitions in exercise 5.

a DSD = Direct store delivery
b CM = Category management
c VMI = Vendor-managed inventory
d CRP = Continuous replenishment
e QR = Quick response

7 Complete the job advertisement for a corporate procurement manager with words from the box.

> fulfilment • negotiation • 3PL providers • procurement • command • vendors • supply chain • relationship

We are looking for a proactive and dynamic professional to take care of our strategic procurement and supplier _____¹ management.

Reporting to the Director of Corporate Procurement, the successful applicant will be responsible for managing both internal and external customers and for working with the appointed _____².
While liaising with the _____³ team, _____⁴ , and related stakeholders, you will also be involved in providing business support to optimize finance-logistics processes, order _____⁵, and logistics costs.

Other responsibilities include providing initiatives to help maximize company business profitability and efficiency.

The ideal candidate should have a degree in _____⁶ management or logistics management with a deep understanding and knowledge of the China logistics market.
You should have at least 5 years' experience in a multinational company and you should possess outstanding _____⁷ skills. Based in Macau, excellent _____⁸ of English and Cantonese is a must with Mandarin an advantage.

If you are interested in this role, please send your CV in Word format to …

8 Read the job advertisement again and answer the questions.

1 What area will the new corporate procurement manager head?
2 What are the procurement manager's main responsibilities? List two or three.
3 Who will he/she collaborate with closely in his/her job?
4 What qualifications are expected?
5 What kind of experience is required?

Can you think of other areas which are important in procurement? Discuss with a partner.

9 Three purchasing managers are discussing strategies for negotiating with a supplier. Listen to the discussion and answer the questions.

1. What kind of relationship do they want with the supplier?
2. What would be the benefits of such a relationship?
3. What market position does the company have?
4. What kind of products do they make?
5. What kind of agreement are they interested in?

10 Match the beginnings (1–6) with the endings (a–f) of the sentences from the dialogue.

1. How do you
2. I think we could
3. What are your
4. Yes, and I also suggest telling them
5. In my opinion it would also be important
6. Good idea. And why don't we

a. to point out that we're interested in establishing a long-term agreement.
b. that this a good opportunity to associate with a brand like ours.
c. feel about that?
d. lower costs considerably.
e. say that it's their chance to enter the pharmaceutical market?
f. thoughts on that, Gisele?

ASKING FOR OPINIONS

What do you think?
How do you feel about that?
What are your thoughts on that?
Do you agree?

GIVING OPINIONS/MAKING SUGGESTIONS

I suggest that we …
In my opinion we should …
Perhaps we should …
Why don't we …?

AGREEING

That's a good idea.
That sounds good.
I agree.
That's right.

Useful phrases **U**

ACTUAL AND CURRENT

Did you know

Actual and **actually** are used to describe the real situation, or to point out some additional information.
We expected the consignment to arrive in 3 days, but it actually (really) took 5 days.

We use the words **current** or **currently** to describe events happening now or at the moment.
Amazon.de provide you with details on the current (present) status is of your delivery.

11 You have received the following email from the purchasing department in your company. Work out a few suggestions and reply to this email.

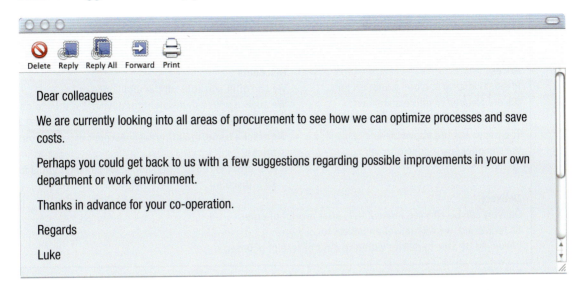

Dear colleagues

We are currently looking into all areas of procurement to see how we can optimize processes and save costs.

Perhaps you could get back to us with a few suggestions regarding possible improvements in your own department or work environment.

Thanks in advance for your co-operation.

Regards

Luke

12 Work with a partner: suggest these points and comment on your partner's suggestions.

PARTNER FILES Partner A File 03, p. 72
Partner B File 11, p. 73

13 A Spanish courier company receives a quotation for packing labels and consignment notes. Put the words or phrases into the correct order to make sentences. The first parts have been done for you.

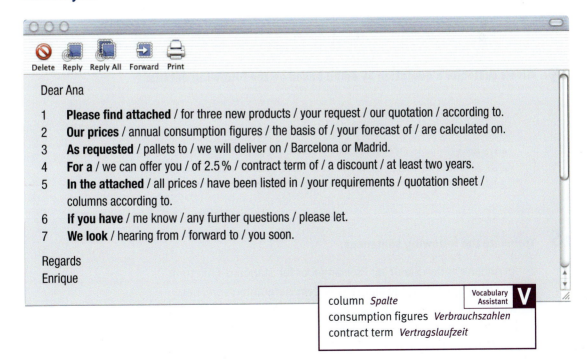

Dear Ana

1 **Please find attached** / for three new products / your request / our quotation / according to.
2 **Our prices** / annual consumption figures / the basis of / your forecast of / are calculated on.
3 **As requested** / pallets to / we will deliver on / Barcelona or Madrid.
4 **For a** / we can offer you / of 2.5 % / contract term of / a discount / at least two years.
5 **In the attached** / all prices / have been listed in / your requirements / quotation sheet / columns according to.
6 **If you have** / me know / any further questions / please let.
7 **We look** / hearing from / forward to / you soon.

Regards
Enrique

Vocabulary Assistant
column *Spalte*
consumption figures *Verbrauchszahlen*
contract term *Vertragslaufzeit*

QUOTATIONS

When giving a customer a quotation it is necessary to include details on a number of things e. g. prices, discounts, and delivery terms.

Here are some useful phrases for quotations:

Prices
Please find attached our quotation for ...
We are pleased to quote as follows.
We can quote you a gross/net price of ...
The prices quoted above include ...
We can offer you a price of ... per ...

Discounts
We can offer you 10 % off the retail price.
We allow a 2 % cash discount for payment within 30 days.
Our prices are subject to a 25 % trade discount off net price.
We grant a trade/quantity/cash discount of ... % on our list prices.
If your order exceeds 2,000 items, we can offer you a further 10 % discount.

Delivery
Delivery can be effected immediately after receipt of order.
As requested, we will deliver on pallets to ...
We would be able to deliver within 10 days of receipt of order.

14 Match the beginnings (1–6) with the endings (a–f) of the sentences.

1 For orders exceeding 500 pieces,
2 We grant a cash discount
3 The prices quoted
4 As requested, we
5 Our prices are subject
6 The net price

a will deliver on pallets to Rotterdam.
b to a 25 % trade discount off net price.
c we grant a discount of 5 %.
d of this article is £ 25.00.
e above include transport charges.
f of 3 % on our list prices.

to be subject to *einer Sache unterliegen*
to exceed *überschreiten*   to grant *gewähren, bewilligen*

15 Give a customer a quotation by email based on the following details.

> GPS system 'Road Navigator TX-2300'
> Price: $ 975.00
> more than 10 items: additional 8 % discount
> price includes 15 % VAT
> delivery within 6 days of purchase order

16 Translate the following sentences.

1 Im Anhang finden Sie unser Preisangebot für Standard-Etiketten.
2 Ich schlage vor, dass Sie morgen mit dem Lieferanten sprechen.
3 Wir können Ihnen einen Rabatt von 10% auf den Nettopreis anbieten.
4 Die oben genannten Preise verstehen sich inklusive Transportkosten.
5 Die Waren werden vom Lager zum Einzelhändler geliefert.

Offload

Read the article and answer the questions.

Strategic sourcing in procurement

Most companies and governments today are under increasing pressure to operate more efficiently. And many of them are realizing that effective procurement can reduce costs, improve processes and increase productivity. In the past few years *strategic sourcing* has become a frequently used approach in this context.

But what is *strategic sourcing*? To put it simply, it means that companies are adopting a new strategy for how they buy services and products.

Strategic sourcing is a systematic process of analyzing expenditures, internal and external influences, and finding out what kind of supplier relationships are necessary to help achieve the company's goals. Before the company decides to purchase a product or service, *strategic sourcing* is used to consider the total cost of a product or action, not just the price alone.

In the past, many purchasing managers neglected the fact that low purchase cost does not necessarily mean low total cost. In a *strategic sourcing* process other costs are examined as well e.g. the cost of purchasing, transport, support, maintenance, and disposal.

Leading companies have realized how much they can benefit from *strategic sourcing*, and many have already achieved impressive cost reductions.

Vocabulary Assistant
to adopt sth *etw anwenden*   approach *Methode, Herangehensweise*   disposal *Entsorgung* expenditure *Ausgaben*   neglect *vernachlässigen*

Over to you

- What do you think of the strategic sourcing approach?
- How are goods purchased in your company?
- Do you buy goods for the company? What is the standard procedure?

4 Modes of transport

Upload

Match the pictures of transport and handling equipment (a–f) with the words (1–6)

a _____

b _____

c _____

d _____

e _____

f _____

1 swap-body
2 container ship
3 straddle carrier
4 road-railer trailer
5 river barge
6 LGV (large goods vehicle)

1 Match the different types of freight traffic (1–6) with the definitions (a–f).

1 multimodal ☐
2 piggyback ☐
3 intermodal ☐
4 unaccompanied ☐
5 block train ☐
6 single-wagon ☐

a The driver does not stay with his road vehicle during transport by rail or ferry.
b Goods are transported in the same loading unit or vehicle using different modes of transport. The handling of the freight itself is not necessary when changing modes.
c A single shipper uses a whole train which is run directly from the loading point to the destination. No assembling and disassembling is required.
d Carriage of goods by at least two different modes of transport, e.g. shipping by motor lorry and aircraft.
e Train is formed out of individual wagons or sets of wagons which have different origins and different destinations.
f Combines road and rail transport: whole motor lorries, trailers or swap-bodies are carried by rail.

2 **Two employees of a forwarding company are comparing transport modes for a shipment from western China to Shanghai. Listen and correct the information in the table.**

	inland waterways	road	rail (express service)
speed in days	7	4	2
cost	low	compared with barge: 60% higher	compared with road: 40% higher
flexibility	high	very high	low

3 **Complete the sentences with the correct form of the words in brackets. Then listen again to check.**

1 How long would it take by barge? – Normally about six days, but it often takes _____ (long) if the weathers bad.

2 It's cheap – it's actually _____ (cheap) of all the transport options.

3 It would only take four days to ship by truck, but the cost would be about 50% _____ (high) than by barge.

4 Rail would definitely be _____ (fast) than the truck option if we use the express service that takes three days.

5 But it would also be _____ (expensive) than shipping by road – transport costs are about 40 % higher.

6 And then perhaps we'd have to use the standard train, which is much _____ (slow).

Answer these questions.

1 Why is the barge option not very flexible?
2 What do they decide to do at the end of their discussion?

MAKING COMPARISONS — *Useful phrases*

When comparing two or more things we use comparative adjectives. The comparative form is **-er** for short adjectives with one syllable, and two-syllable adjectives ending in **-y**.
  Transport by sea is **cheaper** than transport by air.
  Steel is **heavier** than paper.

We use **more** + adjective with longer words.
  Shipping goods by road is **more expensive** than shipping them by rail.
  Some transport modes are **more reliable** than others.

Some adjectives have irregular forms.
  good / well – better   Our rates are **better** than theirs.
  bad / badly – worse   Their service is **worse** than ours.
  far / further – furthest   This shipment will travel **further** than the last one.

---

4 Work in pairs. Compare different transport modes using some of the adjectives in the box.

Example: *I think shipping goods by rail is faster than sea transport.*

adjectives	transport modes
slow / fast	rail
expensive / cheap	air
safe	road
suitable	sea
reliable	river
environmentally friendly	pipeline

Vocabulary Assistant
reliable *zuverlässig*
suitable *geeignet*

5 Match the pictures (a–d) with the names (1–4).

a _____

b _____

c _____

d _____

1 gantry crane
2 ISO container
3 reach stacker
4 transtainer

6 Now complete the descriptions of intermodal transport and handling equipment with the verbs from the box.

fitted • straddle • mounted • loading • attached • reach • handle • piling • made • move

1 A piece of machinery used for _____¹ and unloading containers from ships onto trucks or rail wagons and vice versa. It is rail-mounted and can _____² at least four railway tracks. It is motorized and can _____³ parallel to the ships side.

2 A special type of device which is able to _____⁴ very heavy loads. It is used for transferring swap-bodies and containers from rail wagons to trucks and vice versa. It has four legs _____⁵ with wheels and a spreader beam which can span a wide area. It can be _____⁶ on rails or rubber tyres and is able to straddle several rows of containers.

3 A kind of fork lift truck used in container handling. It is equipped with a spreader beam and a lifting arm and can be used for lifting containers and _____ 7 them on top of each other. It is very flexible and has a high stacking and storage capacity as it is able to _____ 8 beyond the first row of containers to lift a container.

4 A rigid box _____ 9 of steel which is very common in intermodal freight transport. It can be used for transport by sea, rail, air, and road. It is available in many different versions and sizes. For example, there are open-top and flat-rack versions. Some of them have wheels or a bogie _____ 10 to them. The most common lengths are 20, 40, and 45 feet. It is made to the specifications of the International Standards Organization.

> **Vocabulary Assistant**
> bogie *Drehgestell (für Schienenfahrzeuge)*   device *Gerät*
> rail-mounted *auf Schienen montiert*   rigid *starr, fest*
> spreader beam *Containertraverse*   to straddle *überspannen, übergreifen*

7 Replace the underlined words with verbs from the box that have the same meaning. Use the correct verb forms.

stack • come • run • fix • attach • lift • fit

1 This type of crane is used for <u>raising</u> containers.

_____

2 Containers <u>are available</u> in a variety of versions and sizes.

_____

3 It's a heavy-duty fork lift truck <u>equipped</u> with a spreader beam.

_____

4 With this device you can <u>pile</u> containers on top of each other.

_____

5 Some containers have a bogie <u>fixed</u> to them.

_____

6 This device is <u>mounted</u> on rails.

_____

7 The crane is motorized and able to <u>move</u> alongside the quay.

_____

8 An employee of a transport company presents some container options to a potential customer. Listen and complete the table with the missing information.

	Type of container	suitable for transport of
1		
2		
3	tanktainer	
4		
5	flat-rack	

9 Listen again and complete the sentences.

> level • tarpaulin • frame • machinery • lashing • removed • controlled • plugs

1 It comes with a timber floor and has various _____ devices to secure the load.

2 These lashing points are located horizontally at floor _____.

3 It is temperature-_____ and is particularly suitable for cargo that needs regulated or cool temperatures.

4 This is a standard container _____ with a tank fitted inside.

5 As an extra, we also offer tank containers with electric _____ in case the cargo needs cooling or heating during transport.

6 It comes with a PVC _____ cover instead of a roof panel to allow loading from the top.

7 The doors can be _____ to make loading easier.

8 We recommend this special type of container for the transportation of heavy _____ and pipes.

Now label the different types of containers 1–5

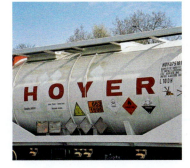

1 _____   2 _____   3 _____

4 _____   5 _____

> **Vocabulary Assistant** V
> electric plug *Steckdose, Elektroanschluss*
> lashing *Verschnüren, Befestigung*   perishables *verderbliche Waren*
> pipe *Rohr*   roof panel *Dachplatte*   tarpaulin *Plane, Verdeck*   timber floor *Holzboden*

> **CONTAINER FEATURES**   Useful phrases U
> We recommend this type of container for …
> It is particularly suitable for …
> It comes with …
> As an extra, we also offer …
> It has … for loading

10 Describe the container features to a partner using words from this unit.

PARTNER FILES Partner A File 04, p. 72
Partner B File 12, p. 73

11 Sort the goods under the correct heading.

meat • steel pipes • crude oil • fresh produce • industrial boilers • seafood • alcohol • dairy products • tractors • chilled or frozen foodstuffs • harmful chemicals

perishable cargo	non-perishable cargo	heavyweight and overwidth cargo

Can you think of other types of goods? Discuss in a small group.

12 Now say which of the following containers you would recommend for the different types of cargo from exercise 11.

a reefer
b flat-rack container
c tank container

13 Complete this crossword puzzle on transport modes with words from the unit.

Across
1 Another word for rubbish.
4 A device for lifting heavy loads.
6 Another word for ship.
7 The opposite of soft or flexible.

Down
2 Another word for pipe.
3 A container for liquids is a _____ container.
4 Kept cool, but not frozen.
5 A container fitted with a cooling system.

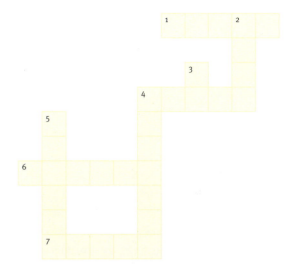

14 Translate the following sentences.

1 Für sperrige Fracht empfehlen wir diesen Container.
2 Die Transportkosten sind 30 % höher als mit der Bahn.
3 Dieses Fahrzeug wird benutzt, um Paletten aufeinander zu stapeln.
4 Wie lange würde es dauern, diese Sendung nach Berlin zu transportieren?
5 Dieser Container ist besonders für verderbliche Waren geeignet.

Read the article and answer the questions.

Freight Transport Logistics in Europe – the key to sustainable mobility

Europes transport policy has been characterized by liberalisation and harmonization over the years. This has slowly shaped the transport system into what it is today. Globalization and the concept of wider Europe create further challenges. The fast growth of freight transport – driven to a large extent by economic decisions – contributes to growth and employment but also causes congestion, accidents, noise, pollution, increased reliance on imported fossil fuels, and energy loss. Infrastructure resources are limited and any disruption in the supply chain (i.e. energy) has necessarily a negative impact on the EU economy. Without adequate measures, the situation will continue worsening and increasingly undermine Europe's competitiveness and the environment that we all live in.

To overcome such problems, Europe's transport system needs to be optimized by means of advanced logistics solutions. Logistics can increase the efficiency of individual modes of transport and their combinations. As a result, fewer units of transport, such as vehicles, wagons, and vessels should carry more freight. Impact on the environment will decrease accordingly.

Rail and inland waterways need to be modernized. Air freight should be more closely integrated in the system. The positive development of short sea shipping should be accelerated. Deep-sea shipping and its hinterland connections need to be enhanced. Shifts to more environmentally friendly modes must be achieved where appropriate, especially on long distance, in urban areas, and on congested corridors.

At the same time each transport mode must be optimized. All modes must become more environmentally friendly, safer, and more energy efficient. Finally, co-modality, i.e. the efficient use of different modes on their own and in combinations, will result in an optimal and sustainable utilization of resources.

Vocabulary Assistant **V**
accelerate *beschleunigen*   accordingly *entsprechend*   appropriate *angemessen, geeignet*   challenge *Herausforderung*   congestion *(Verkehrs-) Stau*   disruption *Unterbrechung*   enhance *verbessern*   sustainable *nachhaltig*   undermine *untergraben*

Over to you

- Do you also have to deal with growing freight traffic in your country?
- How do you think transport systems could be improved?
- How do you think intermodal transport systems can make freigh

5 Planning and arranging transport

Upload

Make a list of all the different factors that would influence your choice of transport method for a shipment. Complete the diagram below.

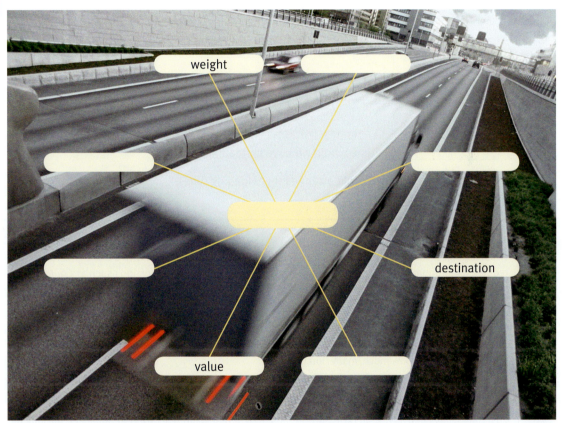

weight

destination

value

1 Listen to the telephone dialogue and answer the questions.

1. What are the two different rail transport options?
2. When do they want to ship?
3. Where will the shipment go?
4. Which train option is recommended for large volume shipments?
5. What would make transport cheaper?
6. How much time will they have for loading the rail wagons?

2   Complete the sentences with the words from the box. Then listen again to check.

> if you like • recommend • an alternative • could you • how much • also consider • calling about • would be • more suitable • suggest that

1. I'm _____ the train options described on your website.
2. _____ tell me a bit more about them?
3. What _____ the best rail option for us?
4. For large volumes, I would _____ using block train transport.
5. If you want to ship smaller quantities, the single-wagon option would be _____.
6. If flexibility is important, I would _____ you book the flexitrain block train option.
7. As _____, I can suggest single-car transport, which is even more flexible.
8. In that case we should _____ the other block train options.
9. _____ time would we have for loading?
10. At least 7 hours, but we could arrange longer loading times _____.

MAKING ENQUIRIES

When asking for information we always use polite language. We often start with a more general request for information before we ask more specific questions. Indirect questions such as *Could you tell me how much it would cost?* are more polite than direct questions e.g. *How much would it cost?*

I'd like to ask/enquire about …
I'm calling about … (on the telephone)
I'm writing about/with regard to … (in an email or letter)
Could you tell me how much/many/long/often …?

ADVISING THE CUSTOMER

Customers may need advice on transport options, freight and insurance rates, shipping and packing details, the route, details regarding weight, dimensions, and measurements.

For this consignment I would recommend/suggest using air transport.
I recommend/suggest that you ship the goods by road.
We/You should also consider air transport for …
That depends on your specific requirements.

OFFERING ALTERNATIVES

Sometimes you need to provide the customer with several alternatives before a decision can be made.

Another option would be to …
Of course it would also be possible to … (instead).
Alternatively, you/we could …

3 Here are some more phrases. Sort them under the correct heading.

A Customer enquiries	B Advice and recommendations	C Offering alternatives

I (would) need some information regarding …
In that case I recommend/suggest that you use/ship …
I think the best option would be to …
If you prefer …, we could also arrange …
Could you let me have some information about …?
We can provide/arrange/ship … if you like.
As an alternative, we can offer you …
What would be the cheapest/fastest/safest/most convenient way/option?

4 Match the beginnings of the sentences (1–6) with the endings (a–f).

1 I would need some information
2 Could you let me know
3 In that case I suggest that you
4 For a consignment this size I
5 Of course it would also be
6 We can also arrange transport

a would recommend rail transport.
b by courier if you prefer.
c regarding loading times.
d what the transit times are?
e possible to ship by express service instead.
f use the cheaper sea freight option.

5 Work with a partner. Follow the steps below and practise making enquiries and giving advice. Use phrases from this unit.

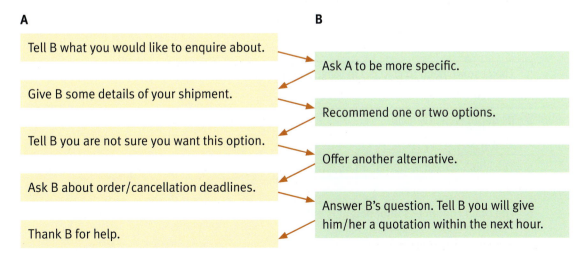

UNIT 5 Planning and arranging transport

6
Listen to a shipping agent describing one of the containers available. Complete the missing details and label the drawing with the words from the box.

height • payload • length • tare weight • width • gross weight

Type of container: 40 ft open top

1 _____ : 4,030 kg

2 _____ : 32,500 kg

3 maximum _____ : 28,470 kg

Internal measurements:

4 _____ : 12.02 m

5 _____ : 2.35 m

6 _____ : 2.32 m

(Container dimensions shown: 2.32 m, 2.35 m, 12.02 m)

7
Listen again and note the non-metric measurements the agent mentions.

1 tare weight: _____

2 internal length: _____

3 internal height: _____

> **Vocabulary Assistant**
> gross weight *Bruttogewicht*
> payload *Zuladung*   tare weight *Leergewicht, Tara*

8
Rewrite the sentences.

Example: The container is 6 metres long.
The length of the container is six metres. (Or: *The container's length is 6 metres.*)

1 The package weighs 45 kg.

_____

2 This seagoing vessel is about 30 m wide.

_____

3 The case we need to ship is 1 m long, 50 cm wide and 35 cm high.

_____

4 Its depth is nearly 3 cm.

_____

5 The ship's length is more than 65 m.

_____

6 The open container's door height is 7 ft 10 in.

_____

9 What do these abbreviations stand for?

1. ft _____
2. kg _____
3. oz _____
4. cm _____
5. lb _____
6. cu yd _____
7. m^2 _____
8. 1" _____
9. pt _____
10. gal _____

10 Put the words from above into the correct column in the table. Complete the table with other measures and weights you can think of.

	metric	non-metric
length		yard (yd)
weight	gram (g)	
surface	square millimetre (mm2)	
volume		
capacity		fluid ounce (fl oz)

11 Describe the measurements and weight of a container to your partner. Use phrases from this unit.

PARTNER FILES Partner A   File 05, p. 72
Partner B   File 13, p. 73

TALKING ABOUT NUMBERS, SIZE, WEIGHT, AND DIMENSIONS

Useful phrases U

Numbers
When dealing with consignment details it is often necessary to talk about numbers.

We write a comma to show thousands (but we don't say it!):
  235,000   two hundred and thirty-five thousand

We use a point to show decimals:
  1.5   one point five

We use the word and after hundreds:
  185   one hundred and eighty-five

When arranging transport, we need to give details about the size and weight of the consignment to be shipped.

Size
Our consignment is 3 by 2 by 2.5 metres.
This box measures 2 by 1.5 by 2.5 metres.
Its measurements are 20 by 85 by 60 centimetres.

Weight
The empty container weighs 5,000 kg.
The net/tare/gross weight of the container is … kg/tons.
The container's maximum payload is …

Dimensions
The box is 40 cm high/long/wide/deep.
Its/The height/length/width/depth is 40 cm.

Remember:
This container is almost six **metres/feet** long (**not** six **metre/foot**!)
But: It's a twenty-**foot** container. (**not feet**!)

UNIT 5 Planning and arranging transport

12 **Listen to the dialogue between a forwarder and a customer asking for a shipping quotation. Then say whether the statements are true (T) or false (F) according to the dialogue.**

1. Karla Hanssen needs a quotation for air freight to the United Arab Emirates.
2. They want to ship cooling units to Abu Dhabi.
3. The consignment consists of 18 boxes.
4. They want to ship from Sweden.
5. The units should be picked up on August 6th.
6. Martin will call back within the next two hours.

13 **Listen again and complete the missing details in the online quotation form.**

Quotation form

Company name:	_____ 1		
Contact:	Karla Hanssen	Tel No:	0046 890265030
Email address:	khanssen@coolair.se	Fax No:	0046 890265039

Shipping information

Point of origin:	_____ 2		
Destination:	_____ 3		
Method of transport:	Air	Number of units/items:	_____ 4
Pick-up date:	_____ 5	Delivery date:	_____ 6

Freight information

Volume (m³):	30.31 m³	Total weight (kg):	_____ 7
Dimensions (cm):	170 cm high, 145 cm wide and 82 cm deep		
Type and nature of goods:	_____ 8		

Special requirements

Hazardous:	_____ 9
Other:	must arrive by _____ 10

Vocabulary Assistant

to get back to sb *sich wieder bei jdm melden*
non-hazardous *ungefährlich*
premises *Gelände*

14 Work with a partner. Write an email asking for a quotation. Include the information from the order form above.

> **REQUESTING A QUOTATION** — Useful phrases
>
> We/I need a quotation for a shipment to …
> Please quote for (the supply/transport of) …
> Please send us a quotation for …
> Please quote your lowest prices for …
> Your quotation should include detailed information on freight and insurance rates, delivery terms, delivery date, and terms of payment.

15 Put the words in the right order.

1. a shipment / send / us / a quotation / please / for / to Madras
2. state / delivery date / please / in your quotation / your earliest
3. let us / could / the following / please / have a quotation / including / details / you ?
4. a part truck load / shipping rates / what / your / for / to Birmingham / are ?
5. on sailing times / your quotation / detailed information / should / and insurance rates / also include
6. the following consignment / please / for / of / quote / the transport

16 Translate the following sentences.

1. Eine andere Möglichkeit wäre, die Ware per LKW zu transportieren.
2. Ich werde mich so schnell wie möglich wieder bei Ihnen melden.
3. Das Paket wiegt 25 kg.
4. Bitte unterbreiten Sie uns ein Angebot für folgende Lieferung.
5. Die maximale Zuladung beträgt 1,5 Tonnen.

Service Printing & Graphics, Inc.
REQUEST FOR PRICE QUOTE

COMPANY INFORMATION

Company _____ Date _____

Contact _____ PO# _____

Phone _____ Fax _____

Email _____

JOB SPECIFICATIONS

Offload

Read the article and answer the questions.

In this week's issue of our GLOBAL TRADE magazine we offer some expert advice on how to successfully ship goods abroad from Hank Wilcox. As the export manager for Jonston Cosmetics, Hank oversees the distribution of cosmetic products to more than 40 countries worldwide. Overseas trade and logistics issues play a major role in the company's business.

▶ *How do you successfully manage shipping logistics at Jonston Cosmetics?*

I think it's most important to work with good freight forwarders. So before we actually choose a freight forwarder, we check whether their service level comes up to our standards.

▶ *What exactly does that mean?*

Well, it means that we only want to work with forwarders who meet certain requirements. One thing that's really important is reliability. We need to be 100 per cent sure that our consignments are delivered to the customer at the right time. We also expect a high level of communication and co-operation between the forwarder and ourselves. And our forwarders must be able to provide flexible transport solutions at short notice.

▶ *And what about transport costs?*

The price is also important obviously, but as I said, there are other things to consider such as quality of service, handling of paperwork and advice. We usually ask for four quotations for each shipment.

▶ *What about all the documentation required in overseas trade?*

We have a team of experienced logistics people who discuss the best possible freight options with the customer and handle all the paperwork. Documentation is really very important, especially if things go wrong. So we always make sure we have copies and duplicates of every document in case something is lost.

▶ *Consignments can easily be damaged in transit. Are your customers aware of that?*

Yes, we always advise our customers on the risks and offer them the most suitable insurance for their consignments. Unfortunately, handling damage is quite common so it's always a good idea to insure a consignment. And insurance is less expensive than most people would expect; it usually costs between one and two per cent of the consignment's value.

Vocabulary Assistant

at short notice *kurzfristig*   duplicate *Zweitausfertigung*   insure *versichern*   reliability *Zuverlässigkeit*

Over to you

- Do you have any experience in dealing with freight forwarders?
- Does the text mention everything a 'good' forwarder should be able to do? Can you add other aspects?
- If you had to choose a forwarder, what criteria would be most important for you?
- In what case would you recommend freight insurance?

6 Shipping goods

Upload

Do you know what these markings represent? Discuss with a partner. Try to label the shipping markings with the correct words.

1 _____   2 _____   3 _____   4 _____

5 _____   6 _____   7 _____   8 _____

Do you know any other markings?

1 Here is an extract from a manual providing rail loading instructions. Complete the sentences with words from the box.

> carefully • attention • overhanging • sure • place • examine • secure • instructions • fit • distribute • exceeded • diagonally

1. _____ vehicle carefully.
2. Do not place items _____ across the wagon.
3. When loading is complete, ensure that it fully complies with the _____ given in our Rail Instructions Manual.
4. Examine load carefully and make _____ it is undamaged and suitable for loading.

5 _____ longer, heavier pieces on the bottom of the load.
6 Make sure that load is _____.
7 Ensure vehicle is _____ to be loaded.
8 Strap _____ loads.
9 When checking the vehicle, give special _____ to door securing mechanisms.
10 Examine vehicle and load _____ after loading.
11 _____ load as evenly as possible and make sure wheels are evenly loaded.
12 Check whether vehicle capacity has not been _____.

> **Vocabulary Assistant**
> to comply with sth *mit einer Sache übereinstimmen*   evenly *gleichmäßig*
> to strap *festschnallen, festzurren*

2 Now match the correct sentences with the instructions below.

a before loading: *1,* _____   b during loading: _____   c after loading: _____

3 Match the beginnings of the sentences (1–8) with the endings (a–h).

1 Remove protruding   a prevent movement.
2 Cover the damaged wall   b on pallets.
3 Secure the load to   c vertically.
4 Fill empty   d staples or nails.
5 Replace damaged pallets   e spaces between products.
6 Align the load   f loading is complete.
7 Stack the boxes   g of the container.
8 Seal the container after   h with new ones.

> **AVOID AND PREVENT**   *Useful phrases*
>
> We use **avoid** when we wish to express a desire to keep oneself away from something or to try not to do something. It is followed by a noun or a gerund.
>   Most delivery companies avoid using the seas where there are dangers of piracy. (keep away from)
>
> We use **prevent** when we want to express a desire to stop somebody doing something or something from happening. It implies that we will take an action to achieve this. The structure we use is to prevent (something) FROM and the verb in the gerund form.
>   We acknowledge our mistake and assure you that we will do all we can to prevent it from happening again. (We will take appropriate action to stop it)

UNIT **6** Shipping goods | **47**

> **EXPLAINING HOW TO DO SOMETHING**
>
> When explaining how to do something, you can use the imperative form of the verb. Use the infinitive without to, like this:
> **Examine** the load carefully.
> **Do** not overload the vehicle.

4 Complete this email about an urgent shipment with prepositions from the box.

by • on • with • in • out • to • between • of

Sonja

I'm afraid there is a problem _____¹ the scheduled deliveries _____² France next week. Our customer GLP Pharma in Brest has just informed me that they are already _____³ of stock and need an urgent delivery of the 5 mg 30 and 90 piece packs this week instead _____⁴ next week. If possible, we must try to make one partial delivery _____⁵ Wednesday (or as soon as the packaging is finished) of the 5mg 30 packs.
We need a direct truck _____⁶ our production plant in Germany and Brest. If we can ship the first part on Wednesday morning, the truck should arrive _____⁷ Brest on Thursday afternoon.
The second delivery should be made on Friday with the rest of the 5mg 30 and the 90 packs. As the products are needed _____⁸ Monday, the truck must be unloaded in Brest on Saturday or Sunday.
Please let me know if there are any problems!

Regards
Jon Frederikson
Logistics Manager

---

5 Sonja and Jon are discussing the urgent delivery over the phone. Listen and answer the questions.

1 Can they use one of their usual forwarding agents?
2 How long would the fastest delivery service take?
3 Would express delivery be a good option?
4 Why is it not possible to deliver at the weekend?
5 What does Jon want to do next?

> **Vocabulary Assistant**
> HGV driving ban *LKW-Fahrverbot*
> partial delivery *Teillieferung*

6 Put the words in the order they are mentioned in the dialogue. Then listen again to check.

1 really / here / I think / a problem / we've / got
2 use / this shipment / our / for / one / unfortunately / we can't / of / regular forwarders
3 we / smaller / this / deliveries / means / partial / that / would / have several

4 have to / a lot more / and / as / we'd / pay / a result
5 Saturdays and Sundays / because of / deliver / we / can't / at the weekend / driving ban / on / the HGV
6 problems / this delivery / no idea / I / would / cause / so many / had

---

INFORMING SOMEONE ABOUT PROBLEMS *Useful phrases* **U**

Telling someone that something cannot be handled in the way it was planned or that something has gone wrong can be difficult. That's why it is important to stay calm and use polite language. It is usually a good idea to say what the problem is exactly and then explain the situation. We often use beginnings such as *I'm afraid ...* or *I'm sorry, but ...*, even if we are not responsible for the problem.

First, we give a brief introduction and then go on to explain the situation in more detail:
  I'm afraid there is a problem with customs clearance.
  I'm sorry, but there will be a delivery delay.

We may also want to give reasons for the problem:
  The delay was caused by a rail strike in Italy.
  The consignment has to be repacked because the carton is damaged.
  There was a delay because of bad weather.
  There was a delay because the weather was bad.

We may also want to talk about contrast, e. g. when we explain that there was a problem, but it hasn't affected the outcome:
  Although the load wasn't secured properly, it arrived intact.
  The load wasn't secured properly, but it arrived intact.
  In spite of the strike, the consignment arrived on time.
  Despite being delayed, the consignment arrived on time.

Sometimes we also need to explain the consequences of certain events:
  The result was that the goods didn't leave the warehouse until Friday.
  As a result, the shipment arrived two hours late.
  There's fog at the airport so the flight hasn't taken off yet.

---

7 Complete the sentences with words from the box.

| so • because • although • due • as a result • despite • because • in spite of |

1 Our customer wants to ship valuable freight, _____ we need to think about insurance.

2 A part of the shipment seems to be damaged _____ of rough handling.

3 _____ the customer needed them urgently, the goods couldn't be delivered earlier.

4 The flight was cancelled _____ to bad weather.

5 The driver had the wrong address. _____ , it took him three hours to deliver the pallets.

6 The consignment arrived on time _____ all the customs formalities at the border.

7 We are unable to ship today _____ we've had problems with our dispatch.

8 _____ being well secured, the load was damaged on arrival.

8 Choose the correct words to complete these sentences.

1 The documents stated the wrong quantities. As a reason/**result**/cause, the shipment was not accepted at the warehouse.
2 The delay was found/noticed/**caused** by an accident on the motorway.
3 When I spoke to the logistics manager, it noticed/saw/**turned** out that they had used different packing material.
4 Unfortunately, we are unable to deliver the consignment **due to**/because/so technical problems in our warehouse.
5 Although/**In spite of**/But the delay, the delivery will still arrive on time.
6 What is the cause/**reason**/result for this delay?

9 You are a freight forwarder. Call your partner to inform him/her about a delivery delay. Use phrases from this unit.

PARTNER FILES Partner A File 06, p. 72
Partner B File 14, p. 73

10 There are six mistakes in this email. Can you correct them?

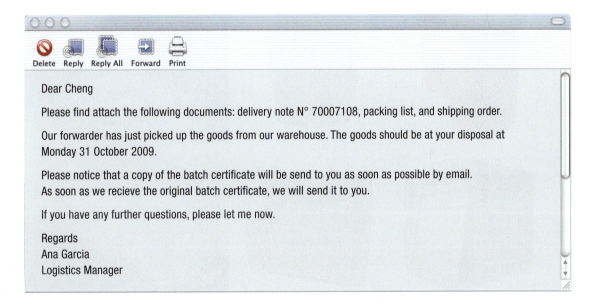

Dear Cheng

Please find attach the following documents: delivery note N° 70007108, packing list, and shipping order.

Our forwarder has just picked up the goods from our warehouse. The goods should be at your disposal at Monday 31 October 2009.

Please notice that a copy of the batch certificate will be send to you as soon as possible by email. As soon as we recieve the original batch certificate, we will send it to you.

If you have any further questions, please let me now.

Regards
Ana Garcia
Logistics Manager

ADVICE OF SHIPMENT
Useful phrases U

When dealing with shipments to customers, it is common practice to advise them that a shipment has been sent. Often details on departure and arrival times, order numbers, and documents are given.

We are pleased to inform you that your order has been dispatched by truck today.
Order N° 3012 has been dispatched by flight BA2379 today.
We are pleased to advise that your order N° 23/1346 was shipped on board the vessel 'Ocean Line'.
The consignment is due to arrive in Sydney on August 25*th*.
The above order has been handed over to our forwarding agents today.
The consignment will be delivered to your warehouse in Brussels.

11 Write a similar email informing a customer about dispatch.

Include the following information:
1 The order number.
2 When the consignment was sent.
3 How the consignment was shipped (road, air, rail, sea).
4 Where it will be delivered.
5 When it will arrive at the customer's site.

12 Match the words (1–5) with the pictures (a–e).

1 bale
2 chest
3 barrel/cask
4 drum
5 crate

a

b

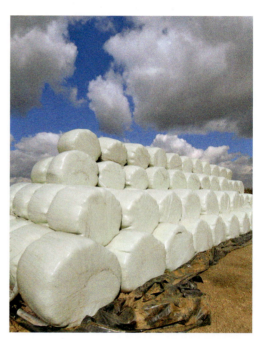

c   d   e

13 Now match the items in exercise 12 with the correct definition.

a Large cylindrical container with a flat bottom and top. It is made of wood and is used for liquids.
b Wooden box made of wooden slats. It can be open or closed and is used for packing goods.
c Large package of presspacked goods (often raw material), which is tightly bound, wrapped, and banded.
d Sturdy box with a lid which is made of metal and often used for storage.
e Cylindrical metal container for liquids.

Vocabulary Assistant
bound (to bind) *gebunden*
slat *Holzlatte*   sturdy *robust, stabil*

14 USTF, international freight forwarders based in Chicago, give some shipping instructions on their website. Complete the sentences with words from the box.

> mark • clearance • withstand • weight • appointed • exhibitor • importing • individually

Shipping Instructions

As the official international freight forwarder _____ [1] by EXPO CHICAGO, we will co-ordinate all international shipments and arrange customs _____ [2] for this event. Please carefully read the following information regarding shipping requirements for _____ [3] goods into the US.

Packing and Marking

1 Ensure that all boxes are securely packed in order to _____ [4] handling by carriers and onsite contractors.

2 Clearly _____ [5] all cartons, cases, or crates on two sides.

3 If you ship your goods in a container, make sure that all cartons are _____ [6] marked and labelled in the following manner:

ADRESS:

Name of _____ [7]:

Number of stand:

Case number (…) of (…)

Total _____ [8] in kg:

15 Translate the following sentences.

1 Bitte stellen Sie sicher, dass die Ladung nicht beschädigt ist.
2 Leider gibt es ein Problem mit dem Lieferdatum.
3 Der Auftrag ist heute an unseren Spediteur übergeben worden.
4 Wir müssen die EU Gesundheits- und Sicherheitsbestimmungen einhalten.
5 Der Flug wurde wegen technischer Probleme gestrichen.

Read the article and answer the questions.

Chaos at Heathrow's New Terminal 5

When Heathrow's Terminal 5 was officially opened by the Queen in March 2008, operator BAA said that it would put the airport at the cutting edge of global travel.

The complex, which cost £4.5bn, includes 50 new aircraft stands, a large car park as well as rail and underground links to London. It is designed to handle 12,000 bags an hour.

BAA claimed that checking in for flights would be simplified for up to 30 million passengers a year by online check-in, fast baggage dropping facilities and sophisticated baggage handling.

Two weeks later, on launch day, however, dozens of flights in and out of the new terminal had to be cancelled due to a breakdown of the baggage handling system. By the end of the first day, hundreds of passengers were left stranded at the airport and there was a backlog of more than 15,000 bags.

What had gone wrong?
On launch day problems started almost immediately, when staff and passengers had trouble locating car parks. Delayed opening of check-in then led to long queues. Additionally, workers in the baggage sorting area had problems logging on to the computer system or could not handle the RMS (Resource Management System), which allocates baggage handlers to load or unload aircraft.

As the check-in staff were not aware of the situation, they continued to add luggage to the system. As a consequence, check-in had to be suspended in the afternoon.

An aviation analyst later explained that the backlog of baggage was mainly caused by problems with the terminal's three-stage baggage processing system.

The first stage, the fast bag drop-off, was working as planned, but the second stage, an underground conveyor system, had become clogged up because baggage workers were not able to remove the bags quickly enough at the other end.

BA said that they knew the first day would be critical because of the size and complexity of the move into Terminal 5, and that they were working hard to resolve these issues.

Vocabulary Assistant

allocate *zuordnen*   at the cutting edge *innovativ, auf dem neusten Stand*   baggage dropping *Gepäckaufgabe*   backlog *Rückstand*   clogged up *verstopft*   queue *Schlange*   sophisticated *hochentwickelt*   suspend *aussetzen, anhalten*

Over to you

- What are the main logistics problems mentioned in this article?
- Have you ever experienced similar problems at an airport?
- How important is logistics for an airport?

Warehousing and storage

Upload

Look at the pictures of warehouse equipment. Match the pictures (a–f) with the words (1–6).

1 hand pallet-truck ☐
2 tote bin ☐
3 fork-lift truck (CB truck) ☐
4 roll-cage pallet ☐
5 (Euro pallet or UK) pallet ☐
6 trolley ☐

1 Read the text describing warehouse areas and label the areas with words from the list.

> sortation • marshalling and dispatch • receiving • collation and value-added services • back-up storage • order picking

First of all, there is the _____ ¹ area. That's where all incoming goods arrive and documentation is checked and recorded. Goods are often unpacked or repacked here to make their format more suitable for warehouse handling.

The _____ ² area holds most of our warehouse inventory.

In the _____ ³ area the goods are selected in the right quantities, that means the quantities required by the customer. Here we also break bulk. That means, for example, after receiving goods in large quantities (e.g. pallets), we need to pack them in smaller separate units for the customer.

In the _____ ⁴ area we deal with smaller order sizes. Sometimes several orders have been batched together to simplify the picking process and now need to be sorted down to individual orders.

After picking, the goods are consolidated and made ready for dispatch. Depending on the customer's requirements the goods may be packed into cartons or cases or they are wrapped (i.e. stretch-wrapping or shrink-wrapping). Some warehouses also provide special services such as labelling. This part of warehouse operations is called _____ ⁵.

The final stage in warehouse operations is the _____ ⁶ area. The goods are brought together to form vehicle loads and are then loaded onto vehicles for onward dispatch.

> **Vocabulary Assistant V**
> collation *Zusammenstellung (von Aufträgen)*
> marshalling *Bereitstellung*   order picking *Kommissionieren*

2 **Match the warehouse areas (1–5) to the activities that take place in them (a–f).**

1 dispatch
2 collation
3 reserve storage
4 order picking and sortation
5 receiving

a goods are brought together for loading and transport
b where the goods are kept until required
c the goods are selected and put together in the units required by the customer
d complete orders are packed and wrapped
e the goods are prepared for warehouse operations

3 **Match the verbs (1–8) from the text in exercise 1 to the correct definitions (a–h).**

1 label
2 repack
3 handle
4 select
5 batch
6 sort
7 wrap
8 load

a put goods on a pallet or vehicle
b provide specific information on the product itself or the packaging
c deal with
d pick or choose
e put several things together
f pack in special material for protection
g put into new units or formats
h arrange in a special way or order

UNIT 7 Warehousing and storage

> **THE PASSIVE** — Useful phrases
>
> When describing processes, the passive voice is often used with modal verbs such as *can, must, may, should,* etc.
> The forks **can be raised** by a simple pump action.
> This system **must be fitted** with detectors.
>
> Or we can use the passive in other tenses e.g. the present perfect tense.
> After the goods **have been checked**, they go into back-up storage.
> The unloading has **been completed**.

4 Complete the sentences using the correct active or passive form of the verbs in brackets.

a After the unit load _____ (check), it goes into automated storage.

b As soon as an appropriate location _____ (identify) by the warehouse management system, a put-away instruction _____ (must, issue).

c After the vehicle driver _____ (report) to the gatehouse, the vehicle documentation _____ (check) by staff.

d Then the packages _____ (process) i.e. they _____ (may, label) with bar codes.

e The goods _____ (check) on unloading.

f After that, staff _____ (direct) the driver to an unloading bay or a parking area.

Now put the steps in the goods receiving process in the correct order 1–6.

1 ____ 2 ____
3 ____ 4 ____
5 ____ 6 ____

5 Listen to this extract from a presentation about a new warehouse management system. Now say which of these statements is true (T) false (F).

1 The existing system is not very efficient.
2 They could centralize inventories in one Canadian warehouse.
3 Cycle times can be reduced by at least half.
4 They could reduce warehouse area from four floors to one.
5 Print on demand allows them to print invoices in several languages.

> **Vocabulary Assistant**
> benefit *Nutzen, Vorteil*
> feature *Eigenschaft, Besonderheit*
> ground space *Lagerfläche*
> outdated *veraltet*

UNIT 7 Warehousing and storage

6 **Now listen to the recording again and complete the sentences.**

1 I think this new warehouse area management system WMS 2X would help us cut costs and _____ our processes.

2 One great advantage of WMS 2X is that we could reduce the number of _____ across Canada.

3 Another interesting feature of WMS 2X is customer order _____.

4 Warehouse _____ could be improved as well by transferring departments.

5 WMS 2X would also help us reduce warehouse area and ground _____.

6 This could be achieved by installing an automated storage and _____ system.

7 The new system would also enable us to _____ the material flow at any given moment.

8 This allows printing of labels, brochures and customer _____ in 25 languages.

Useful phrases

TALKING ABOUT ADVANTAGES AND POSSIBLE IMPROVEMENTS

One great advantage is …
The most interesting feature is …
It would help us reduce/increase/improve/optimize …
Another major advantage is/would be …
It would also guarantee/ensure …

---

7 **Work with a partner. Each of you has a warehouse management system. Present the advantages of your system to your partner. Use phrases in the box.**

PARTNER FILES Partner A File 07, p. 72
Partner B File 15, p. 73

8 **Complete the descriptions of typical warehouse equipment and systems. Use the adjectives from the box.**

stackable • mobile • adjustable • suitable • bulky • driverless • rigid • collapsible

1 An automated guided vehicle is a _____ truck which is controlled by computer and electrically powered.

2 IBCs (intermediate bulk containers) made of metal or plastic are _____, but there are also ones made of canvas, which are _____.

3 Cage and box pallets are fitted with corner-posts and sides. They are usually

   _____ .

4 In palletized storage APR, i. e. _____ pallet racking, is used.

5 Some products are not _____ for palletization e.g. expensive electronic items

   or large and _____ items.

6 _____ shelving is often used for smaller products in non-palletized systems.

bulky *sperrig*	**Vocabulary Assistant**

9 Put the steps in this integrated packing location system in the correct order (1–8). Then listen and check.

☐ You scan the barcode of the shipping label.
☐ The system calculates the weight of the package.
☐ You enter the system.
☐ You choose means of transport.
☐ You can put together packages.
☐ The shipping labels are printed.
☐ You can see and access all positions in the container.
☐ The order is complete – system prints delivery note.

| data interface *Datenschnittstelle* | **Vocabulary Assistant** |
| scales *Waage* | |

10 Now listen to the dialogue again and complete the sentences.

1 After the goods have arrived at the packing location, _____ to scan in the barcode of the shipping box.

2 _____ you enter the packing location dialogue.

3 OK. I got that. What is _____ ?

4 Well, _____ you can access all positions in the picking container.

5 _____ the package is complete, the system will automatically calculate the weight.

6 That is _____ . The system will automatically print the shipping labels.

7 And now we _____ of this process.

8 _____ the order has been completed, the delivery note is printed automatically.

DESCRIBING THE STEPS OF A PROCESS — Useful phrases

First(ly)/First of all …
Second(ly) …
The first step/stage (of the process) is …
Then …
After that …

The next step/stage is …
Following that …
Finally …
The last step is …
Once/After X has happened …

11 Work with a partner and describe a process from your own job in your own words. Use phrases from this unit.

12 Complete this crossword with words from the unit.

Across
2 Keep goods in a warehouse.
4 Put on top of each other.
5 Container for smaller products.
6 Select the right items.

Down
1 Form smaller units from larger units (2 words – 5, 4).
2 Put into the right order or package.
3 Another word for article or piece.

13 Translate the following sentences.

1 Die Kartons werden für den Versand fertig gemacht.
2 Ein weiterer großer Vorteil ist Flexibilität.
3 Danach müssen die Paletten auf Fahrzeuge geladen werden.
4 Der erste Schritt ist, den Strichcode einzulesen.
5 Würde uns dieses System helfen, die Lagerkapazität zu erhöhen?

Offload

Read the text about modern warehousing and answer the questions.

Warehousing today

In the past, a warehouse was only seen as a place to store things. It often took up a lot of ground space and goods were usually picked by hand or using a fork-lift truck.

During the last few years, however, the role and the design of the warehouse have radically changed. The warehouse is now considered a critical link between a manufacturing plant and the external world with a strong impact on the performance of the entire manufacturing and logistics system.

Warehouse automation and complex technologies are now used in order to produce effective operations. Many warehouses today are equipped with warehouse management systems (WMS), which automate the product flow throughout the warehouse and maximize the use of warehouse space through effective picking methods, location consolidation and cross docking.

Automated Storage and Retrieval Systems (AS/RS) have been introduced in many warehouses. AS/RS involves high-racking storage with a machine operating within the aisles, serving both sides of the aisle. These systems can pick, replenish, and perform inventory checks without a human operator.

In fully automated systems, conveyor belts are very important as they link the different areas of the warehouse and carry the goods to where they are required: for example between the receiving areas and reserve storage, or between the picking and loading areas.

The warehouse of today would be unthinkable without the barcode. The barcode label on each item provides specific information about the product, which can be transferred to a computer system. This makes it possible to locate the item's position in the warehouse and find it again. By using automated technology, such as barcode scanners and RFID (radio frequency identification), warehouse inventory and product flow can be efficiently managed. Combined with modern IT systems, barcodes enable warehouse staff to track and trace all items in the warehouse at any given time and usually in real time.

 Vocabulary Assistant

aisle *Gang*
consolidation *hier: Zusammenlegung*
conveyor belt *Förderband*   high-racking *Hochregal*
impact *Auswirkung*   performance *Leistung(sfähigkeit)*

Over to you

- How is your company's warehouse organized?
- Do you work in a warehouse yourself?
- How has warehousing changed over the last few years?

8 Documentation and finance

Here are some more abbreviations. They all relate to documentation and finance. Do you know what they mean?

1 B/L   B___l of l_____
2 D/P   Do__u____ts aga____t p__y_____
3 EXW   Ex _____
4 CIF   C___t, in_____, fr_____
5 AWB   Air w___ b____
6 IMO   Int_____t_____ m_____y o__d__
7 B/E   B___l of ex_____
8 L/C   L__t___ of cr_____

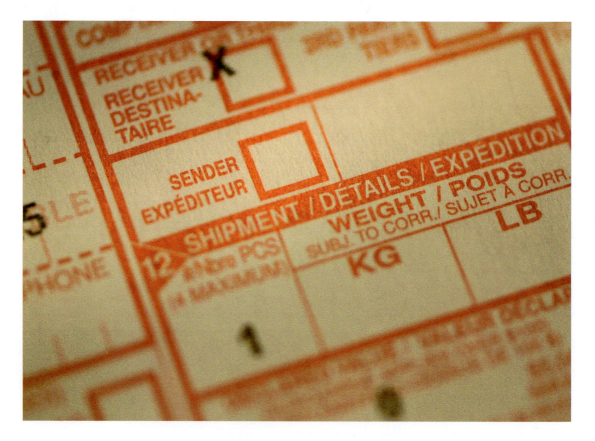

1 Complete this list of documents used in foreign trade with words from the box.

> approved • authority • required • commercial • indicating • draft • receipt • conditions • carriage • hazardous

1 **Commercial invoice**
 A document that contains specific information regarding the goods shipped and the

 _____ agreed between buyer and seller.

2 **Certificate of origin**
 Document used in foreign trade which states where the goods were produced. It is often

 _____ by customs authorities.

3 **Packing list**
 A document which specifies the contents of any form of packaging, e.g. boxes, containers,

 cartons, without _____ the value of the goods shipped.

4 **Air waybill**
 A contract between airline and shipper. It is a shipping document which states the terms and

 conditions of _____ and is also a receipt for the consignment.

5 **Consular invoice**
 A special kind of invoice sometimes required by the importing country. It needs to be

 _____ by an embassy.

6 **Pro forma invoice**
 A _____ invoice which the seller prepares before the actual shipment takes place.

7 **Export licence**
 A document which is granted by a government _____ and states that specified goods can be exported.

8 **Customs invoice**
 A specific document required by customs in some countries e.g. US when importing goods.

 It includes more details than a _____ invoice.

9 **Dangerous goods declaration**
 Certificate prepared by the shipper/consignor which states that _____ goods are handled according to international shipping regulations.

10 **Bill of lading**
 A contract between carrier and shipper which specifies the goods to be shipped and the delivery

 terms. It is also a _____ of shipment and accompanies the goods until

 they reach their destination.

2 **CB GLOBAL SHIPPING, US customs brokers handling an international trade event, provide some instructions on their website. Put the words in the correct order. The first word has been done already.**

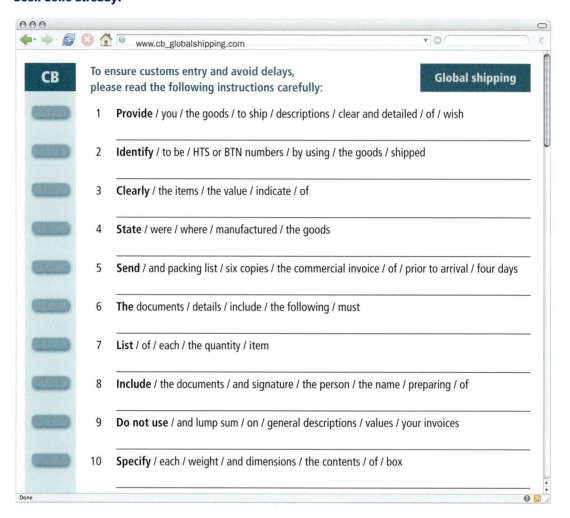

www.cb_globalshipping.com

CB — **Global shipping**

To ensure customs entry and avoid delays, please read the following instructions carefully:

1 **Provide** / you / the goods / to ship / descriptions / clear and detailed / of / wish

2 **Identify** / to be / HTS or BTN numbers / by using / the goods / shipped

3 **Clearly** / the items / the value / indicate / of

4 **State** / were / where / manufactured / the goods

5 **Send** / and packing list / six copies / the commercial invoice / of / prior to arrival / four days

6 **The** documents / details / include / the following / must

7 **List** / of / each / the quantity / item

8 **Include** / the documents / and signature / the person / the name / preparing / of

9 **Do not use** / and lump sum / on / general descriptions / values / your invoices

10 **Specify** / each / weight / and dimensions / the contents / of / box

3 **There is a problem with an urgent delivery. Listen to the three phone conversations and answer the questions.**

17–19

Conversation 1
1 Why is the customer in Iceland upset?
2 Why do they need the consignment so urgently?

Conversation 2
3 What went wrong with the shipment?
4 When does Ms Egbert say she needs the consignment?

Conversation 3
5 When and how will the containers be shipped to Iceland?
6 When should the containers arrive in Iceland?
7 Why could the consignment be rejected at the gate?

Vocabulary Assistant

to be rejected *zurückgewiesen werden*
to be upset *verärgert/bestürzt sein*
to get on to sth *sich um etwas kümmern*
to sort out *lösen, klären*

4 Complete the sentences with words from the box. Then listen again and check.

> get back • the least • very sorry • be OK • just talked • find out • should have • see to • seems that • sorted out • get on

1 Sorry, I have no idea at the moment, but I'll _____ .
2 OK, I'll _____ to this straight away.
3 I've just checked all the documents and it _____ we used the wrong address.
4 I'm _____ about this, Ms Egbert, but I'll do everything I can to get this problem _____ .
5 I'll _____ to you as soon as I've spoken to the forwarder.
6 I've _____ to our freight forwarders here in the UK.
7 That way you _____ them by Friday afternoon.
8 Would that _____ for you?
9 Yes, I'll _____ that.
10 It's _____ I can do for you.

TAKING ACTION AND APOLOGIZING

Useful phrases

After a problem or mistake has been brought to your attention, it is important to deal with it promptly. Note that we tend to use a more formal style in written communication. When responding to a customer, it is a good idea to acknowledge that we are aware of the problem:
  We are replying to your email of April 24th informing us that … (more formal)
  Thank you for informing us about an error in our December statement. (more formal)
  Thanks very much for pointing out the mistake.
  I understand there is a confusion in addresses/delivery dates.

Then we say what we want to do (or have done) to solve the problem. We often use phrasal verbs when talking about taking action:
  We are looking into this matter and will contact you again later today. (more formal)
  I shall/will get in touch with the forwarding agent at once.
  I'll take care of this straight away.
  I'll get on to that now.
  I'll see to this immediately.
  I'll get back to you on that as soon as possible.

We usually also apologize for the problem or mistake:
  We would like to apologize for the inconvenience. (more formal)
  We very much regret this misunderstanding. (more formal)
  I'm very sorry about that.
  Let me apologize for this delay/mistake/error (once again).

5 Complete the sentences with verbs from the box.

look • take care • see to • get on • get in touch • get back

1 I'll _____ to this immediately.
2 Can I _____ to you on that in about half an hour?
3 OK, I'll _____ of that straight away.
4 Fine. I'll _____ with the courier people at once.
5 Thanks for letting me know. I'll _____ this right away.
6 Yes, we'll _____ into the case and call you back tomorrow.

6 Work with a partner to solve a problem. Use phrases from this unit.

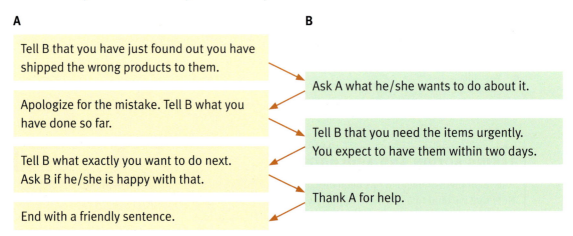

A
- Tell B that you have just found out you have shipped the wrong products to them.
- Apologize for the mistake. Tell B what you have done so far.
- Tell B what exactly you want to do next. Ask B if he/she is happy with that.
- End with a friendly sentence.

B
- Ask A what he/she wants to do about it.
- Tell B that you need the items urgently. You expect to have them within two days.
- Thank A for help.

7 After arranging the express transport with the forwarder, Peter, the logistics manager writes an email to confirm what has been agreed. Choose the correct preposition.

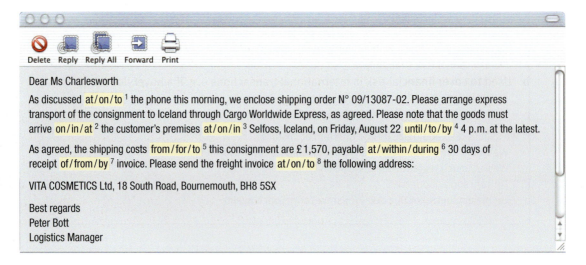

Dear Ms Charlesworth

As discussed at/on/to ¹ the phone this morning, we enclose shipping order N° 09/13087-02. Please arrange express transport of the consignment to Iceland through Cargo Worldwide Express, as agreed. Please note that the goods must arrive on/in/at ² the customer's premises at/on/in ³ Selfoss, Iceland, on Friday, August 22 until/to/by ⁴ 4 p.m. at the latest.

As agreed, the shipping costs from/for/to ⁵ this consignment are £1,570, payable at/within/during ⁶ 30 days of receipt of/from/by ⁷ invoice. Please send the freight invoice at/on/to ⁸ the following address:

VITA COSMETICS Ltd, 18 South Road, Bournemouth, BH8 5SX

Best regards
Peter Bott
Logistics Manager

BY AND UNTIL

Useful phrases

We use the prepositions *by* and *until* to describe different situations:
by = something happens (or should happen) not later than a specific point in time
The consignment must be delivered by Friday.

until/till = something continues up to a specific point in time
The logistics manager will be away until Friday.

8 Complete the sentences with *by* or *until*.

1. I'll make sure that the documents arrive _____ the end of the week.
2. We have to arrange shipment _____ August 4th.
3. I'm afraid there will be delays _____ the beginning of July.
4. They said we would receive the consignment _____ Monday.
5. Call me if there are any problems. I'll be in my office _____ 6.30 today.
6. We require the goods _____ March 15th.

9 Match the payment methods (1–6) with the definitions (a–f).

1. advance payment
2. cash on delivery
3. open account
4. documents against payment
5. documentary credit
6. bank guarantee

Vocabulary Assistant
commitment *Verpflichtung, Zusage*

a Customer pays immediately on receiving the goods. This service is usually provided by the post office.

b Used to cover financial risk in international transactions e.g. if a buyer does not pay.

c The exporter supplies the goods and the importer/customer pays for them at an agreed date in the future.

d Involves the buyer's and the seller's bank. It is a promise made by the opening bank that payment will be made on receiving documents that comply with the terms agreed.

e Also called cash against documents (CAD). It means that the exporter has full control over the documents until payment has been made by the importer.

f Customer/importer has to pay for the goods before they are shipped.

UNIT 8 Documentation and finance

10 Three people are talking about payment methods in their companies. Listen and complete the table.

	Method of payment used	How secure is it for the seller? (very secure, secure, not secure)
Company A:		
Company B:		
Company C:		

LOW RISK
↕
HIGH RISK

> **Vocabulary Assistant**
>
> documentary credit *Dokumentenakkreditiv*
> open account facilities *offenes Zahlungsziel, Zahlung gegen Rechnung*
> to take out insurance *eine Versicherung abschließen*

11 Listen again and say which of these statements are true (T) or false (F) according to the recordings.

1. Most of their European customers expect open account facilities.
2. Open account terms are good for the exporter.
3. They can take out special insurance against the risk of non-payment.
4. A letter of credit is often used for customers you have worked with for a long time.
5. A letter of credit is a very secure payment method.
6. Most customers do not like advance payment.

HANDLING PAYMENT

Useful phrases

It is common to let trading partners know when payment is requested, has been made, or has been received. This is usually done in a short standard email or letter.
More complicated international transactions sometimes require additional information.

Requesting and arranging payment
Please find attached our pro forma invoice for order N° 45-09-23.
We enclose a copy of your invoice. The original will be sent to you together with the documents on settlement of our draft.
We have instructed our bank today to transfer/remit the amount of £6,320 to your account with Royal Bank of Scotland.
Please find enclosed a cheque for $745.55 in payment of your invoice N° 2/08/2457.
We enclose our draft for $23,840 drawn on Pacific Bank, Seattle. Could you please acknowledge receipt?

Acknowledging payment
Thank you for your credit transfer for £4,500 in payment of our July statement.
Our bank has advised us today that your transfer for invoice N° FR 1235 has been credited to our account.
We have received your draft for invoice N° 12349. Thank you for sending it so promptly.

UNIT **8** Documentation and finance | **67**

12 Match the beginnings of the sentences (1–8) with the endings (a–h).

1. We enclose your statement of
2. Our bank informs us that they have received the documents and will transfer
3. Thank you for sending
4. We are pleased to inform you that we have arranged for a
5. Please find enclosed our bank draft for £13,468.40 as
6. We would like to inform you that the amount of £2,567.89 has
7. Please transfer the amount of $2,200
8. As agreed, we are sending you

a. credit transfer through our bank for the amount of $20,000.
b. our invoice for order N° 9089 in duplicate.
c. your draft for invoice N° SR-5602.
d. account as of 30 September.
e. been credited to our account today.
f. to the following account.
g. payment on pro forma invoice No 08/5643.
h. the amount of £8,670 to your account.

13 Look at the words in the box and exercise 11 and use your dictionary (if necessary) to complete the table.

	Verb	Noun
1	remit	
2		transfer
3	receive	
4		draft
5	advise	
6	pay	
7		credit
8	acknowledge	

> **Vocabulary Assistant** V
> to acknowledge sth
> *etw anerkennen, eingestehen, bestätigen*

ACKNOWLEDGE AND CONFIRM
Did you know?

We use **acknowledge** when we recognize that something has happened: When you acknowledge a letter or an email you recognize that it has arrived. We also use acknowledge to accept that something is true.
We would like to acknowledge your letter from last week. (to recognize that it arrived)

We use **confirm** when we verify and restate our intention to do something.
I confirm that I will be at the meeting next Monday (restate my intention after checking the facts)

14 Write a short email to a trading partner.

Partner A File 08, p. 72
Partner B File 16, p. 73

> **DEALING WITH ERRORS AND MISTAKES IN TRADE DOCUMENTS, STATEMENTS AND INVOICES**
>
> When dealing with errors it is important to use polite language. It is also a good idea to make statements less direct and personal by using passive forms and impersonal expressions (e.g. seem and appear).
> It seems/appears that a mistake has been made with regard to the customs invoice.
> There seems to be a discrepancy between the items listed on your statement and the goods delivered.
> When checking your statement, we noted that invoice TX 274 has been debited twice.
>
> It is important to say what we will do or expect the other person to do:
> We are returning your invoice as the 2 per cent discount has not been deducted from the total amount.
> Could you please let us have a corrected/an amended invoice by return?
> Could you make sure that weight and dimensions of the items are specified on the commercial invoice?

15 Say which sentence in each pair is more polite and/or less direct.

1. a You have made an error on the December statement.
   b There appears to be an error on the December statement.

2. a The discount has not been deducted from the total amount.
   b You did not deduct the discount from the total amount.

3. a There is a discrepancy between invoice and packing list.
   b It appears that there is a discrepancy between invoice and packing list.

4. a Could you let us have a corrected invoice?
   b Send us a corrected invoice.

5. a A mistake has been made in invoice N° 09-234.
   b There is a mistake in invoice N° 09-234.

to deduct *abziehen*	Vocabulary Assistant

6. a Use the above bank account number for future transactions.
   b Please make sure that the above bank account number is used for future transactions.

> **DISCOUNT AND REBATE**
>
> A **discount** is a reduction in the normal price of something. The reduction is given AT THE TIME of purchase or payment. Effectively you pay less than the list price.
> *If you pay cash on delivery you get a 5% discount.* (reduction given on payment)
>
> A **rebate** is money we are entitled to claim back AFTER we pay the amount. It is not given at the time of purchase or payment but it is reimbursed at a later date.
> *The company paid too much tax so they are entitled to a rebate.* (paid back after they paid their tax)

16 Translate the following sentences.

1. Bitte geben Sie an, wo die Ware hergestellt wurde.
2. Ich setze mich sofort mit dem Spediteur in Verbindung.
3. Bitte beachten Sie, dass die Sendung bis spätestens 1. Februar ankommen muss.
4. Könnten Sie uns bitte umgehend eine berichtigte Rechnung zukommen lassen?
5. Bitte überweisen Sie den Betrag über € 2150,00 auf folgendes Konto.

Offload

Read these answers to frequently asked questions relating to financial risk in international trade. Answer the questions.

Handling financial risk in international trade

What are the main financial risks for companies doing business overseas?
The first risk area obviously has to do with the customers' credit rating and status. There's always the danger that the customer does not pay for the goods you have supplied. But there are quite a lot of other country-related trade risks which need to be considered.

Could you give some examples?
Well, this could be anything that delays or stops trade or payment e.g. some unexpected economic measures, political unrest, import bans, or breakdown of banking systems in the country you are doing business with.

What can traders do to minimize financial risks?
Before doing business abroad, it is essential to investigate both customer and target country carefully. Check whether the potential customer is solvent, then study your target country's accounting and credit practices and learn something about import and export procedures. To reduce the risk of non-payment, you can take out an export credit insurance policy.

What payment methods would you recommend for exporting goods?
That's a difficult question to answer. The exporter should, of course, always try to minimize financial risk by choosing a secure payment method e.g. advance payment or a confirmed, irrevocable letter of credit. On the other hand, that's not always possible or even desirable.

Why is that?
Well, if you want to do business in a country or market, you have to see what payment facilities your competitors are offering and offer something similar – even if that's not what you really want. And sometimes exporters may decide against secure payment methods such as a letter of credit because the bank charges are high and eat up their profits.

 Vocabulary Assistant

accounting practices *Bilanzierungs-, Buchhaltungspraktiken*
bank charges *Bankgebühren*   competitor *Konkurrent*
measure *Maßnahme*   solvent *zahlungsfähig*   unrest *Unruhen*

Over to you

- What are the main financial risks in foreign trade mentioned in this article?
- How can traders reduce their financial risk?
- Does your company export or import goods? If yes, do you know what methods of payment are used?
- Have you ever heard about payment or credit problems with customers?

Test yourself!

See how much logistics vocabulary you've learned. Use the clues to complete the crossword puzzle.

Across
2 A company which specializes in arranging and handling the transport of goods.
3 Another word for send, used in connection with goods.
4 An offer stating prices and conditions.
8 How much something is worth in money.
9 A wooden base on which goods can be transported.
14 This is where goods are stored.
16 A company which transports goods.
20 A company which provides goods.
21 To send money.
23 To choose or select goods.
24 A document that gives details about the cost of something and is also a request for payment.
26 Another word for freight.
27 A ship used to transport goods on inland waterways.
28 A box made of cardboard.
29 Another word for consequence, e. g. as a …

Down
1 A secure payment method used in international trade. (3 words – 6, 2, 6)
5 A piece of paper providing specific information, either on the product itself or the packaging.
6 A business that sells goods to the end consumer.
7 The weight of goods which can be loaded onto a vehicle.
10 A motor vehicle used for transporting goods.
11 This means that something breaks easily.
12 Another word for buying.
13 Another word for inform.
15 Important document used in international trade. (3 words – 4, 2, 6)
16 A large metal box in which goods are shipped.
17 Another word for get.
18 The opposite of export.
19 Finding an item in transit.
22 The measurement system used in most countries.
25 To put things on top of each other.
26 A device used for lifting heavy goods.

Test yourself! | **71**

Partner A — Partner files

UNIT 1 Exercise 8 — File 01

Job specification for position as store supervisor
- Responsible for store and inventory.
- Make purchase requests for all stocked items that are at minimum.
- Receive and process incoming orders.
- Ensure materials received are in good condition.
- Inform customers of collection or delivery dates.
- Check invoices against orders.

UNIT 2 Exercise 7 — File 02

India Logistics Ltd – International Freight Forwarders
High quality international freight forwarding services from India.
Air and sea freight, distribution services, order management, customs brokerage.
Many years of experience in shipping goods quickly and cost-effectively.
Sophisticated software to prepare documents quickly and correctly.

UNIT 3 Exercise 12 — File 03

1. examine all purchasing processes in the company to see where we can make procurement more efficient
2. sort items to be bought into different categories according to their importance and value
3. develop a system of preferred suppliers (suppliers must meet certain criteria and go through formal approval process)

UNIT 4 Exercise 10 — File 04

Flat-rack container
suitable for: heavy loads, e.g. industrial machinery, pipes
consists of: steel frame with a timber floor, with or without collapsible end walls
loading: from the side up

UNIT 5 Exercise 11 — File 05

20ft standard container

Max. payload:	47,999 lb	21,727 kg
Tare weight:	4,916 lb	2,229 kg
Capacity:	1,172 cu ft	33.18 m³
Inside length:	19 ft 4 in	5.89 m
Inside width:	7 ft 8 in	2.33 m
Inside height:	7 ft 10 in	2.38 m

UNIT 6 Exercise 9 — File 06

A consignment of 35 laptop computers has been delivered to the company's branch in Hanoi instead of Ho Chi Minh City. The distribution centre gave you the wrong address. You have just arranged transport to Ho Chi Minh City by Vietnam Air. The computers should arrive on Friday.

You are a customer in Canada. You are expecting to have something picked up from your premises tomorrow at 9 a.m.

UNIT 7 Exercise 7 — File 07

- invoices are automatically generated
- accurate stock control and warehouse tracking
- hand-held laser scanners provide speed and accuracy
- processing of picked goods

UNIT 8 Exercise 14 — File 08

- You have received pro forma invoice N° 3698 – thank partner B.
- The bank draft for € 6,345 as payment is enclosed.
- Ask for details regarding shipping date and expected arrival of consignment.

Partner B — Partner files

UNIT 1 Exercise 8 — File 09

Job specification for position as distribution manager
- Extensive knowledge of current tariffs, rates, and import and export regulations.
- Monitor shipping operations.
- Hire and train staff.
- Develop business plans.
- Assess warehouse operations and provide feedback.
- Ensure the budget is not overspent.

UNIT 2 Exercise 7 — File 10

Baltic Logistics – Logistics Services
Offices in all three Baltic States.
Air and sea freight, warehousing and distribution services.
Integrated, flexible logistics solutions.
Team of 50 logistics specialists.

UNIT 3 Exercise 12 — File 11

1. reduce the number of suppliers to 10–15
2. use online catalogue for routine items (prices have already been negotiated by the purchasing department)
3. take a close look at existing supplier relationships and think about establishing long-term partnerships with some suppliers of important items

UNIT 4 Exercise 10 — File 12

Bulk container
suitable for: unpackaged dry bulk cargo, e.g. grain
extras: liner bags coated for moisture protection
loading: several spouts and discharge tubes for loading and unloading

UNIT 5 Exercise 11 — File 13

20ft reefer

Max. payload:	45,760 lb	20,756 kg
Tare weight:	7,040 lb	3,193 kg
Capacity:	1,000 cu ft	28.31 m³
Inside length:	17 ft 8 in	5.38 m
Inside width:	7 ft 5 in	2.26 m
Inside height:	7 ft 5 in	2.26 m

UNIT 6 Exercise 9 — File 14

You are the manager of an IT store in Ho Chi Minh City. You were expecting a delivery of 35 laptop computers. You need the computers to arrive by Friday morning.

You have just checked the documents for a shipment to a customer in Canada and noticed that there is something wrong. The pallet height is not the same as in the packing list and the shipping labels are not correct either. You need to wait for correct documents. That's why pick-up time must be changed to 12.30 tomorrow.

UNIT 7 Exercise 7 — File 15

- preparation and printing of shipping labels
- inter-warehouse transfers
- handling of returns
- scanning of case label barcodes

UNIT 8 Exercise 14 — File 16

- You have received bank draft as payment on invoice N° 3698 – thank partner A.
- The consignment is due to leave Liverpool on 1 September, expected arrival in Churchill, Canada, on September 15th.

Answer key

UNIT 1

page 5

Upload
Suggested answers:
purchasing, procurement, transportation, maintenance, distribution, inventory management, stock control, storage, freight forwarding

1
1. storage
2. delivery
3. provide
4. distribution
5. support, maintenance

page 6

2
1. provision
2. to store
3. support
4. to deliver
5. to distribute
6. maintenance
7. to transport
8. to purchase

3
1. maintenance
2. deliver
3. purchasing
4. provide
5. transports
6. store

4 1d 2f 3e 4a 5c 6b

page 7

5
1. freight forwarder
2. shipping operations manager
3. warehouse manager

6
1. organize
2. dealing
3. negotiating
4. arrange
5. make sure
6. advise
7. liaise
8. ensure

page 8

7 1e 2a 3h 4g 5b 6d 7f 8c

page 9

9
1. provide
2. inform, about
3. ensure
4. check
5. organize
6. train

page 10

11
1. My company provides an excellent delivery service.
2. How much cargo do you handle per year?
3. We do not ship chemical products to other countries.
4. The warehouse manager is also responsible for vehicles and machinery.
5. Does this vendor supply car parts to foreign companies?
6. A freight forwarder usually arranges documentation for companies.

13 Across
4. cargo
5. stock
6. liaise

Down
1. plan
2. quote
3. monitor
5. ship

14
1. I work for a large / major international shipping company / freight forwarder.
2. We have an extensive distribution network in Europe.
3. What do you do (for a living)?
4. He works in purchasing.
5. I take care of customs clearance on behalf of my customers/clients.

UNIT 2

page 12

Upload
1. full container load
2. third-party logistics
3. heavy goods vehicle
4. distribution centre
5. less than container load
6. electronic data interchange
7. value-added services
8. radio frequency identification
9. International Standards Organization
10. Global Positioning System

1 1c 2e 3a 4d 5b 6h 7g 8f

page 13

2
1. receipt
2. equip
3. carriage
4. assemble
5. locate

3
1. solutions for full container loads and less than container consolidated freight, sea
2. home textiles, road
3. consolidated air freight forwarding, air

4
1. transport companies
2. shipping lines
3. fleet of vehicles
4. documentation
5. provider
6. air carriers

page 14

5
1. major
2. specialize
3. customized
4. happy
5. provide
6. range

page 15

8
1. 3PL in the past
2. Change in logistics concepts
3. Changing logistics requirements for manufacturers
4. New challenges for 3PL
5. Today's role of major providers

page 16

9
1. True
2. False: outsourcing single segments to different providers is not efficient.
3. False: pressure on prices has led to a decrease in margins.
4. True
5. True

10 1c 2a 3f 4b 5d 6e

page 16/17

11 Maxwell
payment:	credit processing
documentation:	literature fulfillment
product assembly:	–
packing/packaging:	pick and pack
other services:	returns processing

Sichuan
payment:	–
documentation:	import/export cargo customs clearance
product assembly:	kitting
packing/packaging:	packaging services, export packing & crating
other services:	–

GLX
payment:	–
documentation:	–
product assembly:	bundling/unbundling
packing/packaging:	polybagging & shrink wrapping
other services:	labelling, recycling

page 17

12
1. True
2. False: log on by selecting your town or region.
3. False: you can check records for up to 90 days.
4. True
5. False: you can't cancel orders online.
6. True

page 18

13 1f 2a 3e 4b 5c 6d

14
1. mobile phone
2. enter
3. RFID
4. tag
5. device
6. GPS-based
7. track
8. digital

15
1. We offer / provide customized / tailor-made solutions for your transport business.
2. With a mouse click you can download documents in pdf format.
3. Our team will be happy to assist you.
4. It allows you to plan deliveries and keep track of your consignments.
5. To make price requests, please log on to our website.

UNIT 3

page 20

Upload
1a 2b 3a 4a 5b

1 1c 2f 3e 4a 5d 6b

page 21

2
1. False: it's called CRP.
2. True
3. True
4. False: three years.
5. True
6. False: 15 %.

3
1. replenishment
2. lead times
3. stock
4. point
5. retailer
6. generated
7. data interchange
8. schedule
9. inventory
10. processing

page 22

4 1c 2f 3a 4d 5e 6b

5
1. is monitored
2. is often used
3. are transferred; are delivered
4. is identified; is co-ordinated
5. are categorized

page 23

6 a3 b5 c1 d4 e2

7
1. relationship
2. 3PL providers
3. procurement
4. vendors
5. fulfilment
6. supply chain
7. negotiation
8. command

8
1. strategic procurement and supplier relationship management
2. manage internal and external customers, optimize processes, order fulfilment and logistics costs
3. with the procurement team
4. degree in supply chain management or logistics management
5. minimum of five years in a multinational company, languages

page 24

9
1. more co-operative relationship, strategic partnership
2. lower costs considerably and work more efficiently
3. market leader
4. pharmaceutical products
5. long-term agreement

10 1c 2d 3f 4b 5a 6e

page 25

11 Suggested answer:
Dear Luke
We have talked about possible cost savings in purchasing in our team. We also think it would be a good idea to discuss this in more detail.
We feel there would be a lot of saving potential in some areas, especially in supplier management.
In our opinion we should:
1. choose our suppliers more carefully
2. establish stricter standards for our suppliers
3. co-operate more closely with some of our important suppliers (to achieve better results).
I'll call you next week to give you some more details on that.
Regards
Mike

13
1. Please find attached our quotation for three new products according to your request.
2. Our prices are calculated on the basis of your forecast of annual consumption figures.
3. As requested we will deliver on pallets to Barcelona or Madrid.
4. For a contract term of at least two years we can offer you a discount of 2.5 %.
5. In the attached quotation sheet all prices have been listed in columns according to your requirements.
6. If you have any further questions please let me know.
7. We look forward to hearing from you soon.

page 26

14 1c 2f 3e 4a 5b 6d

15 Suggested answer:
Dear …
Please find attached our quotation for our GPS system 'Road Navigator TX-2300'.
We can offer you a price of $975.00 per item including VAT at 15 %.
If your order exceeds 10 items, we can offer an additional discount of 8 %. Delivery will be made within 6 days of receipt of purchase order.
If you have any further questions, please let me know.
Best regards

16
1. Please find attached our quotation for standard labels.
2. I suggest that you speak to the supplier tomorrow.
3. We can offer you a 10% discount on the net price.
4. The prices quoted above include transport charges.
5. The goods are delivered from the warehouse to the retailer.

UNIT 4

page 28

Upload
a3 b2 c4 d5 e6 f1

page 28/29

1 1d 2f 3b 4a 5c 6e

page 29

2 speed in days
inland waterways: 6
road: 4
rail (express service): 3

cost
inland waterways: low
road: 50 % higher than barge
rail (express service): 40 % higher than truck

flexibility
inland waterways: low
road: very high
rail (express service): low

page 29/30

3
1. longer
2. the cheapest
3. higher
4. faster
5. more expensive
6. slower

Suggested answers:
1. Infrequent sailings: there are barges twice a week.
2. Check with the customer first to find out what they want.

page 31

5 a2 b4 c3 d1

page 31/32

6
1. loading
2. straddle
3. move
4. handle
5. fitted
6. mounted
7. piling
8. reach
9. made
10. attached

page 32

7
1. lifting
2. come
3. fitted
4. stack
5. attached
6. fixed
7. run

page 33

8
1. general purpose: dry cargo
2. reefer, refrigerated: delicate cargo and perishables
3. tanktainer: liquids
4. open top: bulky cargo
5. flat-rack: heavy machinery and pipes

page 33/34

9
1. lashing
2. level
3. controlled
4. frame
5. plugs
6. tarpaulin
7. removed
8. machinery

1. reefer container
2. tanktainer
3. general purpose container
4. flat-rack container
5. open-top container

page 34

11 perishable cargo: meat, fresh produce, seafood, dairy products, chilled or frozen foodstuffs
non-perishable cargo: crude oil, alcohol, harmful chemicals
heavyweight and overwidth cargo: steel pipes, industrial boilers, tractors

page 35

12
a. reefer: perishable cargo
b. flat-rack container: heavyweight and/or overwidth cargo
c. tank container: non-perishable cargo

13 Across
1. waste
4. crane
6. vessel
7. rigid

Down
2. tube
3. tank
4. chilled
5. reefer

14
1. For bulky freight/cargo we recommend this container.
2. Transport charges/costs are 30% higher than by rail.
3. This vehicle is used to stack pallets on top of each other.
4. How long would it take to ship this consignment to Berlin?
5. This container is particularly suitable for perishables.

UNIT 5

page 37

Upload
Suggested answers:
size, dimensions, type of goods, infrastructure, time factor/speed/urgency, nature of the goods, security

1
1. block train, single-wagon
2. next month
3. London, UK
4. block train
5. if they could plan well ahead
6. at least 7 hours

page 38

2
1. calling about
2. Could you
3. would be
4. recommend
5. more suitable
6. suggest that
7. an alternative
8. also consider
9. How much
10. if you like

page 39

3
A. I (would) need some information regarding …
Could you let me have some information about …?
What would be the cheapest / fastest / safest / most convenient way / option?
B. In that case I recommend / suggest that you use / ship …
I think the best option would be to …
We can provide / arrange / ship … if you like.
C. If you prefer … , we could also arrange …
As an alternative, we can offer you …

4 1c 2d 3f 4a 5e 6b

page 40

6
1. tare weight
2. gross weight
3. payload
4. length
5. width
6. height

7
1. tare weight: 8,880 pounds
2. internal length: 39 foot 5 inches
3. internal height: 7 foot 7 inches

8
1. The weight of the package is 45 kg.
2. The width of this seagoing vessel is about 30 metres.
3. The measurements of the case we need to ship are 1 m (long) by 50 cm (wide) by 35 cm (high).
4. It is nearly 3 centimetres deep.
5. The ship is more than 65 metres long.
6. The open container's door is 7 foot 10 inches high.

page 41

9
1. foot
2. kilogram
3. ounce
4. centimetre
5. pound
6. cubic yard
7. square metre
8. inch
9. pint
10. gallon

10

	metric	non-metric
length	millimetre (mm) centimetre (cm) metre (m) kilometre (km)	inch (1 in) foot (ft) yard (yd) mile (m)
weight	gram (g) kilogram (kg) tonne (t)	ounce (oz) pound (lb) short ton (t) US long ton UK
surface	square millimetre (mm²) centimetre (cm²) metre (m²) kilometre (km²)	square inch (sq in) foot (sq ft) yard (sq yd) mile (sq m)
volume	cubic millimetre (mm³) centimetre (cm³) metre (m³)	cubic inch (cu in) foot (cu ft) yard (cu yd)
capacity	litre (l)	fluid ounce (fl oz) pint (pt) quart (qt) gallon (gal)

page 42

12
1. True
2. False: they are going to Dubai.
3. False: there are 15 boxes.
4. True
5. False: August 3rd.
6. True

13
1. Cool Air
2. Stockholm, Sweden
3. Dubai, United Arab Emirates
4. 15
5. August 3rd
6. August 6th
7. 150 kg x 15 = 2,250 kg
8. Cooling units
9. no
10. August 6th

page 43

14 Suggested answer:
Please send a quotation for the shipment of 15 cooling units from Stockholm, Sweden to Dubai, United Arab Emirates. The units can be picked up August 3rd and must arrive no later than August 6th. We would like them transported by air. The units weigh 150 kg each. They are 170 cm high, 145 cm wide, and 82 cm deep. Your quotations should include detailed information on freight and insurance rates, delivery terms, and terms of payment.
Best regards

15
1. Please send us a quotation for a shipment to Madras.
2. Please state your earliest delivery date in your quotation.
3. Could you please let us have a quotation including the following details?
4. What are your shipping rates for a part truck load to Birmingham?
5. Your quotation should also include detailed information on sailing times and insurance rates.
6. Please quote for the transport of the following consignment.

16
1. Another option would be to ship the goods by road/truck.
2. I will get back to you as soon as I can.
3. The package weighs 25 kilograms.
4. Please quote for / give us a quotation for the following shipment.
5. The maximum payload is 1.5 tons.

UNIT 6

page 45

Upload
1. Fragile
2. This side up
3. Use no hooks
4. Do not stack
5. Explosive
6. Store away from heat
7. Keep dry
8. Toxic

page 45/46

1
1. examine
2. diagonally
3. instructions
4. sure
5. place
6. secure
7. fit
8. overhanging
9. attention
10. carefully
11. distribute
12. exceeded

page 46

2
a. before loading: 1, 4, 7, 9
b. loading: 2, 5, 8, 11
c. after loading: 3, 6, 10, 12

3 1d 2g 3a 4e 5h 6c 7b 8f

page 47

4
1. with
2. to
3. out
4. of
5. on
6. between

7 in
8 by

5 1 No, they can't.
2 The fastest option takes 48 hours.
3 No, because they have very limited loading capacity.
4 Because of the HGV driving ban on Saturdays and Sundays.
5 He wants to call GLP and then get back to Sonja.

page 47/48

6 1 I think we've really got a problem here.
2 Unfortunately, we can't use one of our regular forwarders for this shipment.
3 This means that we would have several smaller partial deliveries.
4 We'd also have to pay a lot more as a result.
5 We can't deliver at the weekend because of the HGV driving ban on Saturdays and Sundays.
6 I had no idea this delivery would cause so many problems.

page 48

7 1 so
2 because
3 although
4 due
5 As a result
6 despite
7 because
8 In spite of

page 49

8 1 result
2 caused
3 turned
4 due to
5 In spite of
6 reason

10 Please find attach**ed** the following documents: delivery note N° 70007108, packing list and shipping order.
Our forwarder has just picked up the goods from our warehouse. The goods should be at your disposal **on** Monday 31 October 2009.
Please **note** that a copy of the batch certificate will be **sent** to you as soon as possible by email. As soon as we **receive** the original batch certificate, we will send it to you.
If you have any further questions, please let me **know**.

page 50

11 Suggested answer:
Order number N° 68809986 was dispatched yesterday, February 13th by rail. It will be delivered to the customer's site in Banbury, UK. It is expected to arrive February 15th before 10 a.m.

12 1 e 2 d 3 b 4 a 5 c

13 1 c 2 d 3 a 4 e 5 b

page 51

14 1 appointed
2 clearance
3 importing
4 withstand
5 mark
6 individually
7 exhibitor
8 weight

15 1 Please ensure / make sure that the load is undamaged.
2 I'm afraid there is a problem with the delivery date.
3 The order has been handed over to our forwarder today.
4 We must comply with EU health and safety regulations.
5 The flight was cancelled due to / because of technical problems.

UNIT 7

page 53

Upload
1 e 2 d 3 f 4 c 5 a 6 b

page 53/54

1 1 receiving
2 back-up storage
3 order picking
4 sortation
5 collation and value-added services
6 marshalling and dispatch

page 54

2 1 a 2 d 3 b 4 c 5 e

3 1 b 2 g 3 c 4 d 5 e 6 h 7 f 8 a

page 55

4 a has been checked
b has been identified, must be issued
c has reported, is checked
d are processed, may be labelled
e are checked
f direct

1 c 2 f 3 e 4 d 5 a 6 b

5 1 True
2 True
3 False: cycle times could be reduced by up to 25 %.
4 True
5 False: she doesn't mention invoices.

page 56

6 1 optimize
2 warehouses
3 service
4 management
5 space
6 tracking
7 track
8 guidelines

page 56/57

8 1 driverless
2 rigid, collapsible
3 stackable
4 adjustable

5 suitable, bulky
6 mobile

page 57

9 1 You scan in the barcode …
   2 You enter the system.
   3 You can see and access all positions …
   4 You can put together packages.
   5 The system calculates the weight …
   6 You choose means of transport.
   7 The shipping labels are printed.
   8 The order is complete …

10 1 the first step is
   2 After that
   3 the next step
   4 following that
   5 Once
   6 actually the next step
   7 come to the last stage
   8 After

page 58

12 **Across**
   2 store
   4 stack
   5 bin
   6 pick

   Down
   1 break bulk
   2 sort
   3 item

13 1 The boxes/cartons are made ready for dispatch.
   2 Another major advantage is flexibility.
   3 After/Following that, the pallets must be loaded onto vehicles.
   4 The first step is to scan the barcode.
   5 Would this system help us increase storage capacity?

UNIT 8

page 60

Upload
   1 B/L   Bill of lading
   2 D/P   Documents against payment
   3 EXW   Ex works
   4 CIF   Cost, insurance, freight
   5 AWB   Air waybill
   6 IMO   International money order
   7 B/E   Bill of exchange
   8 L/C   Letter of credit

page 61

1 1 conditions
   2 required
   3 indicating
   4 carriage
   5 approved
   6 draft
   7 authority
   8 commercial
   9 hazardous
   10 receipt

page 62

2 1 Provide clear and detailed descriptions of the goods you wish to ship.
   2 Identify the goods to be shipped by using HTS or BTN numbers.
   3 Clearly indicate the value of the items.
   4 State where the goods were manufactured.
   5 Send six copies of the commercial invoice and packing list four days prior to arrival.
   6 The documents must include the following details.
   7 List the quantity of each item.
   8 Include the name and signature of the person preparing the documents.
   9 Do not use general descriptions and lump sum values on your invoices.
   10 Specify the contents, weight, and dimensions of each box.

3 1 Because the shipment of both pearls in plastic containers hasn't arrived yet.
   2 Because they want to start packaging on Monday.
   3 It was delivered to the wrong address/customer.
   4 By Monday.
   5 By express cargo.
   6 By Friday afternoon.
   7 Because the address on the documents is wrong.

page 63

4 1 find out
   2 get on
   3 seems that
   4 very sorry, sorted out
   5 get back
   6 just talked
   7 should have
   8 be OK
   9 see to
   10 the least

page 64

5 1 get on
   2 get back
   3 take care
   4 get in touch
   5 see to
   6 look

7 1 on
   2 at
   3 in
   4 by
   5 for
   6 within
   7 of
   8 to

page 65

8 1 by
   2 by
   3 until
   4 by
   5 until
   6 by

9 1f 2a 3c 4e 5d 6b

page 66

10 Company A: open account, not secure
Company B: letter of credit, one of the most secure
Company C: advance payment, the most secure

11
1 True
2 False: they're good for the buyer.
3 True
4 False: it's for new customers.
5 True
6 True

page 67

12 1d 2h 3c 4a 5g 6e 7f 8b

13
1 remittance
2 transfer
3 receipt
4 draw
5 advice
6 payment
7 credit
8 acknowledgement

page 68

15 1b 2a 3b 4a 5a 6b

16
1 Please state where the goods were manufactured.
2 I'll get in touch with the forwarder straight/right away.
3 Please note that the shipment/consignment must arrive by 1 February (at the latest).
4 Could you please let us have an amended / a corrected invoice by return?
5 Please transfer/ remit the amount of € 2,150 to the following account.

page 70/71

Test yourself!

Across
2 forwarder
3 dispatch
4 quotation
8 value
9 pallet
14 warehouse
16 carrier
20 supplier
21 remit
23 pick
24 invoice
26 cargo
27 barge
28 carton
29 result

Down
1 letter of credit
5 label
6 retailer
7 payload
10 truck
11 fragile
12 purchasing
13 advise
15 bill of lading
16 container
17 receive
18 import
19 tracking
22 metric
25 stack
26 crane

Transcript

UNIT 1, EXERCISE 1

Speaker 1 Logistics means that you manage the procurement and movement of goods and the storage of inventory.

Speaker 2 It means the delivery of the goods the customer needs at the right time, in the right place, and of the right quality.

Speaker 3 My definition of logistics is this: it's to plan, organize, and manage operations that provide services and goods.

Speaker 4 Logistics – that's the purchasing, maintenance, distribution, and replacement of material and staff.

Speaker 5 Logistics is the planning and support of operations such as warehousing, inventory, transport, procurement, supply, and maintenance.

UNIT 1, EXERCISE 5

Speaker 1 My job is to organize the transport of goods either by sea, air, road, or rail. An important part of the job is dealing with customer requests about the most suitable mode of transport. My responsibilities also include negotiating good shipping rates with shipping lines and transport companies. I also make booking reservations, that means I book space on a ship, train, lorry, or airplane. Another part of the job is to consolidate a number of shipments under one bill of lading. Apart from that, I have to deal with all the necessary documentation and, in many cases, I arrange customs clearance on behalf of my clients.

Speaker 2 I'm responsible for getting freight and passengers to their destination safely and on schedule. Most of my customers are international transport or shipping companies. In my job I have to make sure that the cargo is not damaged onboard the ship or while loading or unloading. I'm also responsible for financial aspects; that means, for example, I have to keep an eye on the budget and estimate costs. Additionally, I advise customers on shipping rates and prepare quotations for our sales office.

Speaker 3 Generally my job is to know where every piece of stock is at any given moment. When new goods arrive, I check where to put them in the warehouse. For all this, I use modern computer systems and sophisticated hardware and software. Our warehouse management system helps us store and retrieve the goods quickly. Another part of my job is to liaise with departments such as transport and production. Apart from that, I ensure that vehicles, machines, and any other kind of equipment are maintained to a high level.

And last but not least, I take care that health and safety standards are maintained.

UNIT 2, EXERCISE 3

(GFT Global Carrier) Provider 1
We are one of the world's leading transport companies with a freight volume of 600,000 containers per year. As a major non-vessel operating common carrier (NVOCC), we can offer our customers competitive rates with all major shipping lines as well as flexible solutions for different sea freight requirements.
We specialize in solutions for full container loads (FCL) and less than container consolidated loads (LCL).
We also provide our customers with services such as web-based tracking for cargo in transit.

(Home Tex International) Provider 2
As a specialist in home textiles, we can offer our clients customized services to meet their needs. With more than 25 years' experience in the industry and a modern fleet of vehicles, we can ensure fast, safe delivery of your consignments. Our services include order picking, packing, distribution and handling of all transport documentation. Our team will be happy to assist you in all matters regarding your order.

(Cargo Express) Provider 3
Cargo Express is Asia's leading provider of air freight services. Specializing in consolidated air freight forwarding, we can provide you with tailor-made solutions for your air transport requirements. We work closely with air carriers around the world and can offer our customers a wide range of flexible and cost-effective services. These include collection, consolidation, customs clearance, distribution, and online tracking of all cargo movements.

UNIT 2, EXERCISE 5

1. As a major non-vessel operating common carrier, we can offer our customers competitive rates with all major shipping lines.
2. We specialize in solutions for full container loads (FCL) and less than container consolidated loads (LCL).
3. As a specialist in home textiles, we can offer our clients customized services to meet their needs.
4. Our team will be happy to assist you in all matters regarding your order.
5. We can provide you with tailor-made solutions for your air transport requirements.
6. We closely co-operate with air carriers around the world and can offer our customers a wide range of flexible and cost-effective services.

UNIT 2, EXERCISE 12

Speaker 1 **Express Logistics Online Shipping**
With our Quick Online Shipping tool you can find the right service to suit your shipping needs. This online tool allows you to plan

shipments, book collections and deliveries, and keep track of your consignments. Using this system you can also prepare shipping and customs documentation and check shipment records for up to 90 days. To use QOS, simply log on by selecting your town or region from the drop-down menu on the left.

Speaker 2 **Intercargo E-Shipping**
Our web-based booking system offers you an extensive range of e-services designed to simplify your shipping requirements. After registering with E-Shipping, you can make price requests, schedule transport, and obtain real-time shipment information. With this user-friendly tool you can receive quotations for worldwide shipments and place orders. You can also track pick-ups and deliveries. With a mouse click you can also download commercial documents in pdf format.

UNIT 3, EXERCISE 2

Today I'm going to tell you something about CRP. That means continuous replenishment. I'll also explain how it can be used to lower inventory and operational costs and to shorten product lead times.

Let me start by explaining what CRP means. It is a system which is activated by consumer demand and which co-ordinates the flow of information and goods in the logistic chain.

CRP is a sales-based ordering system which works like this: first of all, you decide what products you want to order at what stock level. The system will use this information at the point of sale in the retail store. Then the order is processed at the warehouse. And finally the goods are delivered to the retailer.

To illustrate how this works in practice, I'll give you an example. The leading Russian clothes retailer Young Fashion introduced continuous replenishment three years ago. With the new system, all orders are generated by computers, which process data received from cash registers. The computer program, which is extremely flexible, is called Retail Ordering Assistant. The orders are sent to the warehouse by electronic data interchange, where they are processed. And finally the goods are delivered to the different outlets according to a schedule.

Since the introduction of the CRP system, Young Fashion have managed to cut inventory and transport costs by about 15 % and have reduced lead time to only 18 hours. Moreover, errors in order processing have been reduced considerably by using scanning technology and EDI.

UNIT 3, EXERCISE 9

Robert OK, let's get started. You know that we need to discuss negotiation strategies with one of our medical equipment suppliers today. I suppose we all agree that we are interested in a more co-operative relationship with our supplier, BAF. I think we would definitely benefit from a strategic partnership. How do you feel about that?

Peter I agree. I think we could lower costs considerably and work more efficiently if we co-operated more closely. But we need to think about reasons why they should enter into a partnership with us. What are your thoughts on that, Gisele?

Gisele I think you're right. That's why we should tell them that it will be to their advantage to work with us because we are the market leader.

Peter Yes, and I also suggest telling them that this a good opportunity to associate with a major pharmaceutical brand like ours.

Gisele That sounds good. In my opinion it would also be important to point out that we're interested in establishing a long-term agreement.

Peter Good idea. And why don't we say that it's their chance to enter the pharmaceutical market. So far they haven't had access to this market.

Gisele Yes, good point.

Robert: Excellent. Thanks for your comments. I'll work out a catalogue with the points we have covered today and will send it to you tomorrow.

UNIT 4, EXERCISE 2

Hao Well, basically we have three shipping options: we can use inland waterways, road, or rail.

Ying Right. Let's start with the river barge. How long would it take to ship the consignment by barge?

Hao Normally about six days, but it often takes longer if the weather's bad.

Ying And what about cost and flexibility?

Hao It's cheap – it's actually the cheapest of all the transport options. It's not very flexible though, mainly because there are only infrequent sailings. There are barges to Shanghai twice a week.

Ying OK, let's look at road transport. It would only take four days to ship by truck, but the cost would be about 50 % higher than by barge.

Hao Yes, but wouldn't it be much easier?

Ying That's true. Let's see how this compares with rail. Rail would definitely be faster than the truck option if we use the express service – that takes three days.

Hao But it would also be more expensive than shipping by road – transport costs are about 40 % higher. And the system isn't very flexible. Sometimes it is only possible to book space on the express train a few weeks in advance. And then perhaps we'd have to use the standard train, which is much slower.

Ying So, I think we need to check with our customer first and find out what's most important to them.

UNIT 4, EXERCISE 8

First of all, we offer the general purpose container for any general dry cargo. It comes with a timber floor and has various lashing devices to secure the load. These lashing points are located horizontally at floor level and vertically next to the door corner posts.

Our refrigerated container, called 'reefer', can be used for delicate cargo and perishables. It is temperature-controlled and is particularly suitable for cargo that needs regulated or cool temperatures. With our reefer your cargo reaches its destination in perfect condition. If you want to ship liquids, for example, foodstuffs or chemicals, we can provide you with our 'tanktainer'. This is a standard container frame with a tank fitted inside. As an extra, we also offer tank containers with electric plugs in case the cargo needs cooling or heating during transport.

For bulky cargo we recommend the open-top container. It comes with a PVC tarpaulin cover instead of a roof panel to allow loading from the top. The doors can be removed to make loading easier.

Last but not least, there is our 'flat-rack' container which is especially designed for heavy loads. We recommend this special type of container for the transportation of heavy machinery and pipes.

UNIT 5, EXERCISE 1

Simon	Global Freight Logistics. Simon Dawson speaking.
Paula	Hello, this is Paula Santini from Marmi Italia. I'm calling about the train options described on your website. Could you tell me a bit more about them?
Simon	Yes, of course. What exactly would you like to know?
Paula	We have some new customers in the UK and will need to ship marble and granite to London next month. What would be the best rail option for us?
Simon	That depends. For large volumes, I would recommend using block-train transport. If you want to ship smaller quantities, the single-wagon option would be more suitable.
Paula	I see. How flexible are the various options? I mean, how early would we need to place our order?
Simon	If flexibility is important, I would suggest that you book the flexitrain block train option. It's a bit more expensive, but with that you can place your order up to 24 hours before the actual shipping date. As an alternative, I can suggest single-car transport, which is even more flexible – you can order up to two hours before collection.
Paula	That sounds good.
Simon	Of course, it is always cheaper if you can plan transport well ahead. In that case we should also consider the other block-train options.
Paula	OK. Just one last question: how much time would we have for loading?
Simon	At least 7 hours, but we could arrange longer loading times if you like.
Paula	Thank you very much for your help. I'll get back to you as soon as I have our customers' specific transport requirements.
Simon	Fine. I look forward to hearing from you again. Goodbye.
Paula	Bye.

UNIT 5, EXERCISE 6

OK, so this is one of our larger containers – the 40ft Open Top. Its tare weight is 4,030 kilos, that is 8,880 pounds. Its gross weight is 32,500 kilos. And here are the internal measurements of the container. The Open Top container's length inside is 12 metres – or 39 foot 5 inches. Its internal width is 2.35 m, and its height is 2.32 m – that's 7 foot 7 inches. And the container's maximum payload is 28,470 kilos.

UNIT 5, EXERCISE 12

Martin	IFT International Forwarders, Martin Smith. How can I help you?
Karla	Hello, this is Karla Hanssen from Cool Air, Sweden. I need a quotation for air freight to the United Arab Emirates. I've been trying to complete the online quotation form, but it keeps crashing.
Martin	Sorry about that. We have had some problems with it recently. I'll see if I can retrieve it. You said your name was Hanssen, didn't you?
Karla	Yes, that's right.
Martin	OK, here it is. Well, it's saved some of your details. We can go through the rest of the consignment details over the phone and I'll fill in the quotation for you.
Karla	Thanks, go ahead.
Martin	OK. Um … let's start with the freight details. Could you briefly describe the goods you want to ship?
Karla	They're cooling units and they're going to Dubai.
Martin	OK, so that's non-hazardous material. How many units do you want to ship?
Karla	15 boxes with a gross weight of 150 kg each.
Martin	Right. And the size of each box?
Karla	Each box is 170 cm high, 145 cm wide and 82 cm deep. I think the volume would be about 30m^3.
Martin	OK, let me just check that for you. Hold the line. [Pause] Hello?
Karla	Hi.
Martin	OK, so the volume would be 30.31 m^3 for the whole consignment … Where do you want to ship the goods from?
Karla	Stockholm, Sweden.
Martin	And when would you like the units to be collected at your premises?
Karla	On August 3rd.
Martin	OK, got that. When should delivery be made?
Karla	It's very important that our customer receives the units on August 6th. Would that be a problem?
Martin	I don't think so, but I'll check. Do you have any other special requirements?
Karla	No, just that delivery date.
Martin	OK – I'll get back to you with a quotation within the next two hours. Could you give me your telephone and fax numbers, please?
Karla	Yes, of course. My number is 0046 890265030 and the fax number is 0046 890265039. And my name is Karla Hanssen.
Martin	Thanks very much Ms Hanssen. I'll speak to you soon. Goodbye.
Karla	Thank you. Bye.

UNIT 6, EXERCISE 5

Jon	Jon Frederikson, Export Logistics.
Sonja	Hi Jon, this is Sonja. I'm just phoning about your email.

Jon	Hi Sonja. Thanks for getting back to me so quickly. So what can we do about GLP in France?
Sonja	I think we've really got a problem here. Unfortunately, we can't use one of our regular forwarders for this shipment. I've talked to all of them and the fastest service would take 48 hours.
Jon	Can't we use someone that specializes in express deliveries?
Sonja	Not really. I've checked this option too, but I'm not sure it would work for us because they offer a very limited loading capacity. This means that we would have several smaller partial deliveries. And we'd have to pay a lot more as a result.
Jon	Hmm. What about the weekend delivery? That's possible, isn't it?
Sonja	I'm afraid not. We can't deliver at the weekend because of the HGV driving ban on Saturdays and Sundays.
Jon	Oh dear. I had no idea this delivery would cause so many problems. I'll talk to GLP again and will get back to you later. Thanks for your help.
Sonja	No problem. Speak to you soon. Bye.
Jon	Bye.

UNIT 7, EXERCISE 5

15

OK, let's get started. We are here today to discuss how we can improve our warehouse management system which, as you all know, is outdated and not very efficient. I think this new warehouse area management system WMS 2X would help us cut costs and optimize our processes. Let me give you some of its main features and benefits.

One great advantage of WMS 2X is that we could reduce the number of warehouses across Canada by centralizing the inventories in one single location. This means that we could service all our North American customers from one warehouse.

Another interesting feature of WMS 2X is customer order cycle times. It optimizes processes and can reduce customer order cycle times by up to 25 %. If we manage to improve our processes in this area, we could increase customer satisfaction by getting the goods to them faster.

Warehouse managment could be improved as well by transferring departments now working at different places to one single place. This could involve the areas receiving, order picking, and packing.

WMS 2X would also help us reduce warehouse area and ground space. I think it is another big plus point that we could have just one warehouse floor instead of the four we have now. This could be achieved by installing an automated storage and retrieval system. The new system would also enable us to track the material flow at any given moment.

And one last advantage is the print-on-demand feature. This allows printing of labels, brochures, and customer guidelines in 25 languages.

UNIT 7, EXERCISE 9

16

Peter	OK, this is how the systems works. It's actually quite simple. After the goods have arrived at the packing location, the first step is to scan in the barcode of the shipping box. After that you enter the packing location dialogue.
Mike	OK, I got that. What is the next step?
Peter	Well, following that you can see and access all positions in the picking container.
Mike	I see.
Peter	If you use this function, you can form one or several packages and once the package is complete, the system will automatically calculate the weight using a data interface between the scales and the system.
Mike	Sounds good. What about the shipping labels?
Peter	That is actually the next step. The system will print the shipping label after you have selected the means of transport. And now we come to the last stage of this process. After the order has been completed, the delivery note is printed automatically.

UNIT 8 EXERCISE 3

Conversation 1

17

Simon	Hi Peter. It's Simon here.
Peter	Hi Simon. How are you doing?
Simon	Fine, thanks. Um, listen Peter, I've just had a call from our customer in Iceland. They are very upset because that shipment of bath pearls in plastic containers which was supposed to be delivered this morning, hasn't arrived yet. Do you know anything about this?
Peter	Sorry, I have no idea at the moment, but I'll find out. Do you want me to get in touch with the customer as soon as I know what the problem is?
Simon	Yes, that would be great. The customer says they urgently need the consignment because they want to start packaging on Monday.
Peter	OK, I'll get on to it straight away. Talk to you later then. Bye.
Simon	Bye.

Conversation 2

18

Brit	Bio Beauty Pharma, Brit Egbert speaking.
Peter	Hello Ms Egbert. This is Peter Bott from Vita Cosmetics. I understand there is a problem regarding the shipment of bath pearls you should have received this morning.
Brit	Yes, well … the containers still haven't arrived. What's the problem?
Peter	I've just checked all the documents and it seems that we used the wrong address. Your consignment was delivered to another customer by mistake. I'm really sorry about this, Ms Egbert, but I'll do everything I can to get this problem sorted out. If I talk to our forwarders here in the UK now, I'm sure we'll find a solution.
Brit	OK. But make sure that we have the consignment by Monday, otherwise we'll be in serious trouble.
Peter	Yes, I understand. I'll get back to you as soon as I've spoken to the forwarder.

Conversation 3

19

Peter	Hello, Ms Egbert. This is Peter Bott again. I've just talked to our freight forwarders here in the UK. They'll pick up the containers at the other customer's premises tomorrow morning and get

	them shipped to Iceland by express cargo. That way you should have them by Friday afternoon. Would that be OK for you?
Brit	Yes, that sounds good.
Peter	Excellent. There's just one other thing. As I said before, the address on the documents travelling with the containers is wrong. Could you make sure that your logistics people know that? Otherwise the consignment might be rejected at the gate.
Brit	Yes, I'll see to that. Thanks for your help.
Peter	It's the least I can do. Let me know if there are any other problems.
Brit	I will. Bye.

UNIT 8 EXERCISE 10

Speaker 1 **Open account**

We mainly do business in Europe, where most of our customers expect us to give them open account terms. Obviously, this method of payment is good for the buyers, but not for us as exporters because we don't really have any control over the payment process. We can ask the customer to pay at a certain date or within a certain period, but we can never be sure that they will pay then. To protect ourselves against non-payment or customer insolvency, we usually take out credit insurance.

Speaker 2 **Letter of credit**

With customers we haven't done business with before, we always use a letter of credit. It allows us to agree detailed terms with the buyer, which can't be changed once they have been fixed. Above all, it's one of the most secure payment methods in foreign trade. The buyer's and seller's bank work together and offer the seller a commitment of payment. With a documentary credit like this we can be sure that we'll be paid for the goods we supply.

Speaker 3 **Advance payment**

We're a small company specializing in high quality computer hardware. Our company policy is that customers have to pay up front. That means the customers transfer the money before we ship the hardware to them. Because we're a small business, our cash flow situation doesn't allow us to offer customers longer credit periods. We wouldn't be able to cope with delayed payment or customers not paying at all. For us as sellers, it's the most secure payment method. We know, of course, that most of our customers would prefer other payment facilities.

A–Z wordlist

A

to **accelerate** [əkˈseləreɪt]	beschleunigen	
access [ˈækses]	Zugang, Zugriff	
to **access sth** [ˈækses]	auf etw zugreifen	
account [əˈkaʊnt]	Konto	
account, open ~ [ˌəʊpən əˈkaʊnt]	Kontokorrent, gegen Rechnung	
accounting practices [əˈkaʊntɪŋ præktɪsɪz]	Bilanzierungs-, Buchhaltungspraktiken	
accuracy [ˈækjərəsi]	Genauigkeit	
to **acknowledge sth** [əkˈnɒlɪdʒ]	etw anerkennen, eingestehen, bestätigen	
acronym [ˈækrənɪm]	Abkürzung, Akronym	
adequate [ˈædɪkwət]	angemessen	
adjustable pallet racking (APR) [əˌdʒʌstəl ˈpælət rækɪŋ]	verstellbares Palettenregalsystem	
to **adopt sth** [əˈdɒpt]	etw anwenden	
advance payment [ədˌvɑːns ˈpeɪmənt]	Vorkasse, Vorauszahlung	
advice of dispatch [ədˌvaɪs əv dɪˈspætʃ]	Versandanzeige	
advice of shipment [ədˌvaɪs əv ˈʃɪpmənt]	Verschiffungsanzeige	
to **advise** [ədˈvaɪz]	beraten, raten; unterrichten, mitteilen	
to **agree (on sth)** [əˈgriː]	etw vereinbaren, sich auf etw einigen	
air carrier [ˈeə kæriə]	Luftfrachtführer, Fluggesellschaft	
air freight [ˈeə freɪt]	Luftfracht	
air waybill [ˌeə ˈweɪbɪl]	Luftfrachtbrief	
aisle [aɪl]	Gang	
to **align** [əˈlaɪn]	ausrichten	
to **allocate** [ˈæləkeɪt]	zuordnen, zuweisen, einteilen	
to **amend** [əˈmend]	ändern, abändern	
applicant [ˈæplɪkənt]	Bewerber/in	
to **appoint sb** [əˈpɔɪnt]	jdn beauftragen, bestimmen	
approach [əˈprəʊtʃ]	Methode, Herangehensweise	
appropriate [əˈprəʊpriət]	angemessen, geeignet	
approval process [əˈpruːvl prəʊses]	Genehmigungsverfahren	
as of (date) [əz əv]	per (Datum)	
to **assemble** [əˈsembl]	zusammenstellen, zusammenbauen, montieren	
assembly [əˈsembli]	Zusammenstellung, Montage	
to **assess** [əˈses]	bewerten, beurteilen	
assessment [əˈsesmənt]	Schätzung	
automated [ˈɔːtəmeɪtɪd]	automatisiert, automatisch	
automated storage and retrieval system [ˌɔːtəmeɪtɪd ˌstɔːrɪdʒ ən rɪˈtriːvl sɪstəm]	Automatisches Regalbediensystem	
automation [ˌɔːtəˈmeɪʃn]	Automatisierung	
aviation [ˌeɪviˈeɪʃn]	Luftfahrt	

B

backlog [ˈbæklɒg]	Rückstand
back-up storage [ˌbækʌp ˈstɔːrɪdʒ]	Sicherheitsbestand
bag [bæg]	Gepäckstück, Koffer, Tasche
baggage [ˈbægɪdʒ]	(Reise-)Gepäck
baggage drop-off (point) [ˌbægɪdʒ ˈdrɒpɒf]	Gepäckaufgabe (Stelle)
baggage sorting [ˈbægɪdʒ sɔːtɪŋ]	Gepäcksortierung
bale [beɪl]	Ballen
banded [ˈbændɪd]	zusammengebunden
bank charges [ˈbæŋk tʃɑːdʒɪz]	Bankgebühren
bank guarantee [ˈbæŋk gærəntiː]	Bankgarantie, Bankbürgschaft
barge [bɑːdʒ]	Lastkahn
barrel [ˈbærəl]	(Holz-)Fass
batch [bætʃ]	Charge, Posten, Los, Ladung
batch certificate [ˈbætʃ sətɪfɪkət]	Kommissionierschein
batch size [ˈbætʃ saɪz]	Losgröße
to **batch together** [ˌbætʃ təˈgeðə]	konsolidieren, zusammenbringen
behalf, on ~ of sb [ɒn bɪˈhɑːf əv]	in jds Auftrag, in jds Namen
bendable [ˈbendəbl]	biegsam
benefit [ˈbenɪfɪt]	Nutzen, Vorteil
to **benefit** [ˈbenɪfɪt]	profitieren
bill of lading [ˌbɪl əv ˈleɪdɪŋ]	Frachtbrief, Konnossement
block train [ˈblɒk treɪn]	Ganzzug, Blockzug
body [ˈbɒdi]	Behörde, Körperschaft
bogie [ˈbəʊgi]	Drehgestell (für Schienenfahrzeuge)
bound (to bind) [baʊnd]	gebunden
branch [brɑːntʃ]	Niederlassung
brand [brænd]	Marke
break-bulk [ˈbreɪkbʌlk]	Stückgut
to **break bulk** [ˌbreɪk ˈbʌlk]	Sammelladung/Stückgut aufteilen, umpacken
breakdown [ˈbreɪkdaʊn]	Ausfall, Zusammenbruch
brief [briːf]	kurz, knapp
brochure [ˈbrəʊʃə]	Broschüre, Prospekt
Brussels tariff number (BTN) [ˌbrʌslz ˈtærɪf nʌmbə]	Klassifikationsnummer für Importware
buffer stock [ˈbʌfə stɒk]	Pufferbestand
bulk cargo [ˈbʌlk kɑːgəʊ]	Schüttgut, Massengut, Schüttung
bulky [ˈbʌlki]	sperrig
bulky cargo [ˌbʌlki ˈkɑːgəʊ]	Sperrfracht, Sperrgut
bundling [ˈbʌndlɪŋ]	Bündelung
to **bypass** [ˈbaɪpɑːs]	umgehen, überspringen

C

to **cancel** [ˈkænsl]	stornieren
cancellation [ˌkænsəˈleɪʃn]	Stornierung
canvas [ˈkænvəs]	Leinwand, Segeltuch
capacity [kəˈpæsəti]	Fassungsvermögen, Rauminhalt
cargo [ˈkɑːgəʊ]	Fracht, Ladung
cargo, bulk ~ [ˈbʌlk kɑːgəʊ]	Schüttgut, Massengut, Schüttung
cargo, dry ~ [ˌdraɪ ˈkɑːgəʊ]	Trockenfracht
cargo, heavyweight ~ [ˌheviweɪt ˈkɑːgəʊ]	Schwerlast
carriage [ˈkærɪdʒ]	Beförderung, Transport
carriage, means of ~ [ˌmiːnz əv ˈkærɪdʒ]	Transportmittel
carrier [ˈkæriə]	Frachtführer
carrier, air ~ [ˈeə kæriə]	Luftfrachtführer, Fluggesellschaft
carrier, non-vessel operating common ~ (NVOCC) [nɒn ˌvesl ɒpəreɪtɪŋ ˌkɒmən ˈkæriə]	Schiffsbuchender Verfrachter, Reeder ohne Schiff
to **carry out** [ˌkæri ˈaʊt]	ausführen
case [keɪs]	Kiste, Kasten
cash against documents [ˌkæʃ əgenst ˈdɒkjumənts]	Kasse gegen Dokumente
cash discount [ˈkæʃ dɪskaʊnt]	Skonto
cash on delivery [ˌkæʃ ɒn dɪˈlɪvəri]	(per) Nachnahme
cash register [ˈkæʃ redʒɪstə]	Kasse
cask [kɑːsk]	(Holz-)Fass
category management [ˈkætəgəri mænɪdʒmənt]	Organisation nach Warengruppen
certificate of origin [səˌtɪfɪkət əv ˈɒrɪdʒɪn]	Ursprungszeugnis
chemical [ˈkemɪkl]	Chemikalie
chest [tʃest]	(Metall-)Kiste

chilled	[tʃɪld]	gekühlt
to claim	[kleɪm]	behaupten
to clog up	[ˌklɒg 'ʌp]	verstopfen
collapsible	[kə'læpsəbl]	zusammenklappbar, faltbar
collation	[kə'leɪʃn]	Zusammenstellung (von Aufträgen)
collection	[kə'lekʃn]	Abholung
column	['kɒləm]	Spalte
commercial documents	[kəˌmɜːʃl 'dɒkjumənts]	Handelsdokumente, Handelspapiere
commercial invoice	[kəˌmɜːʃl 'ɪnvɔɪs]	Handelsrechnung, Warenrechnung
commitment	[kə'mɪtmənt]	Verpflichtung, Zusage
to compensate for sth	['kɒmpənseɪt fə]	etw ausgleichen
competition	[ˌkɒmpə'tɪʃn]	Wettbewerb, Konkurrenz
competitive	[kəm'petətɪv]	(Preis:) günstig, (Markt:) umkämpft
competitor	[kəm'petɪtə]	Konkurrent
competitiveness	[kəm'petətɪvnəs]	Konkurrenzfähigkeit
to complement	['kɒmplɪmənt]	ergänzen
to comply with sth	[kəm'plaɪ wɪð]	einer Sache entsprechen, mit einer Sache übereinstimmen
comprehensive	[ˌkɒmprɪ'hensɪv]	umfassend
condition	[kən'dɪʃn]	Bedingung
to confirm	[kən'fɜːm]	bestätigen
confusion	[kən'fjuːʒn]	Verwechslung, Irrtum
congestion	[kən'dʒestʃən]	(Verkehrs-)Stau
consignee	[ˌkɒnsaɪ'niː]	Empfänger/in, Adressat/in
consignment	[kən'saɪnmənt]	Warensendung, Lieferung
consignment note	[kən'saɪnmənt nəʊt]	Frachtbrief, Warenbegleitschein
consignor	[kən'saɪnə]	Versender, Absender, Verlader
to consolidate	[kɒn'sɒlɪdeɪt]	zusammenstellen
consolidation	[kənˌsɒlɪ'deɪʃn]	Zusammenfassen (von Lieferungen), Konsolidieren
consular invoice	[ˌkɒnsjələ 'ɪnvɔɪs]	Konsulatsrechnung, -faktura
consumer goods	[kən'sjuːmə gʊdz]	Konsumgüter
consumption	[kən'sʌmpʃn]	Verbrauch
consumption figures	[kən'sʌmpʃn fɪgəz]	Verbrauchszahlen
container	[kən'teɪnə]	Behälter, Container
contents	['kɒntents]	Inhalt
continuous replenishment (CRP)	[kənˌtɪnjuəs rɪ'plenɪʃmənt]	kontinuierliche Bestandsauffüllung
to contract sth out to sb	[kənˌtrækt 'aʊt]	etw an jdn (einen Subunternehmer) vergeben
contractor	[kən'træktə]	Dienstleister, beauftragte Firma
contract term	['kɒntrækt tɜːm]	Vertragslaufzeit
convenient	[kən'viːniənt]	praktisch, günstig
conveyor belt	[kən'veɪə belt]	Förderband
conveyor system	[kən'veɪə sɪstəm]	Fördersystem
courier	['kʊrɪə]	Kurier(dienst)
crate	[kreɪt]	Holzkiste
crating	['kreɪtɪŋ]	Verpacken (in Kisten)
to credit	['kredɪt]	gutschreiben, kreditieren
credit processing	['kredɪt prəʊsesɪŋ]	Zahlungs-, Rechnungsabwicklung
credit rating	['kredɪt reɪtɪŋ]	Bonitätseinstufung
credit worthiness	['kredɪt wɜːðɪnəs]	Bonität, Kreditwürdigkeit
credit status	['kredɪt steɪtəs]	Kreditwürdigkeit
credit transfer	['kredɪt trænsfɜː]	Überweisung
cross-docking	['krɒsdɒkɪŋ]	Warenumschlag (ohne Zwischenlagerung)
crude oil	[ˌkruːd 'ɔɪl]	Rohöl
customer	['kʌstəmə]	Kunde/in
customer order cycle time	[ˌkʌstəmə ɔːdə 'saɪkl taɪm]	Durchlaufzeit, Bearbeitungszeit eines Kundenauftrags
customer satisfaction	[ˌkʌstəmə ˌsætɪs'fækʃn]	Kundenzufriedenheit
customized	['kʌstəmaɪzd]	maßgeschneidert, dem Kundenwunsch angepasst
customs	['kʌstəmz]	Zoll
customs brokerage	['kʌstəmz brəʊkərɪdʒ]	Erledigung der Zollformalitäten (durch einen Zollspediteur oder Zollmakler)
customs clearance	['kʌstəmz klɪərəns]	Zollabfertigung
customs entry	['kʌstəmz entri]	Zolleinfuhr
customs invoice	['kʌstəmz ɪnvɔɪs]	Zollfaktura, Zollrechnung
to cut costs	[kʌt 'kɒsts]	Kosten senken
cutting edge, at the ~	[ət ðə ˌkʌtɪŋ 'edʒ]	innovativ, auf dem neuesten Stand
cycle time	['saɪkl taɪm]	Durchlaufzeit

D

dairy products	['deəri prɒdʌkts]	Molkereiprodukte, Milchprodukte
to damage	['dæmɪdʒ]	beschädigen
dangerous goods	[ˌdeɪndʒərəs 'gʊdz]	Gefahr(en)güter
dangerous goods declaration	[ˌdeɪndʒərəs 'gʊdz dekləreɪʃn]	Verantwortliche Erklärung (für gefährliche Güter)
data interface	[ˌdeɪtə 'ɪntəfeɪs]	Datenschnittstelle
to debit	['debɪt]	(Konto) belasten, (Geld) abbuchen
decrease	['diːkriːs]	Rückgang, Reduzierung
dedicated	['dedɪkeɪtɪd]	(Mitarbeiter:) engagiert, motiviert
to deduct	[dɪ'dʌkt]	abziehen
deep-sea shipping	[ˌdiːp siː 'ʃɪpɪŋ]	Hochseeschifffahrt
degree	[dɪ'griː]	(Bildung:) Abschluss
delicate	['delɪkət]	empfindlich
delivery	[dɪ'lɪvəri]	Lieferung
delivery note	[dɪ'lɪvəri nəʊt]	Lieferschein
delivery terms	[dɪ'lɪvəri tɜːmz]	Lieferbedingungen
delivery, partial ~	[ˌpɑːʃl dɪ'lɪvəri]	Teillieferung
demand	[dɪ'mɑːnd]	Nachfrage
demanding	[dɪ'mɑːndɪŋ]	anspruchsvoll
department	[dɪ'pɑːtmənt]	Abteilung
depot	['depəʊ]	Lager, Magazin
destination	[ˌdestɪ'neɪʃn]	Ziel, Bestimmungsort
device	[dɪ'vaɪs]	Gerät
digit	['dɪdʒɪt]	Ziffer
digit, double-~	[ˌdʌbl 'dɪdʒɪt]	zweistellig
dimension	[dɪ'menʃn]	Dimension, Abmessung
discharge tube	['dɪstʃɑːdʒ tjuːb]	Entladungsröhre, Ablass-, Ablaufrohr
discount	['dɪskaʊnt]	Rabatt, Skonto
discrepancy	[dɪs'krepənsi]	Unstimmigkeit, Diskrepanz
dispatch	[dɪ'spætʃ]	Versand
to dispatch	[dɪ'spætʃ]	versenden, verschicken
disposal	[dɪ'spəʊzl]	Entsorgung
disruption	[dɪs'rʌpʃn]	Störung, Unterbrechung
distribution	[ˌdɪstrɪ'bjuːʃn]	Vertrieb, Auslieferung
distribution manager	[ˌdɪstrɪ'bjuːʃn mænɪdʒə]	Vertriebsleiter/in
documentary credit	[dɒkjuˌmentri 'kredɪt]	Dokumentenakkreditiv
documentation	[ˌdɒkjumen'teɪʃn]	Dokumente, Unterlagen, Papiere
documents against payment	[ˌdɒkjumənts əgenst 'peɪmənt]	Dokumenteninkasso
to draft	[drɑːft]	(Schriftstück) ausstellen
draft	[drɑːft]	Zahlungsanweisung, Wechsel
to draw a draft	[ˌdrɔː ə 'drɑːft]	einen Wechsel ziehen
driving ban	['draɪvɪŋ bæn]	Fahrverbot
drum	[drʌm]	(Öl-)Fass
dry cargo	[ˌdraɪ 'kɑːgəʊ]	Trockenfracht

E

duplicate ['dju:plɪkət]	Zweitausfertigung
duplicate, in ~ [ɪn 'dju:plɪkət]	in zweifacher Ausfertigung
economies of scale [ɪˌkɒnəmiz əv 'skeɪl]	Kostenersparnis durch Großaufträge
to effect sth [ɪ'fekt]	(Handlung) ausführen
electric plug [ɪˌlektrɪk 'plʌg]	Steckdose, Elektroanschluss
electronic data interchange (EDI) [ɪlekˌtrɒnɪk 'deɪtə ɪntətʃeɪndʒ]	elektronischer Datenaustausch
embassy ['embəsi]	Botschaft
to enclose sth [ɪn'kləʊz]	etw (einem Brief, etc.) beilegen
end-to-end solution [end tu ˌend sə'lu:ʃn]	Komplettlösung
to enhance [ɪn'hɑ:ns]	verbessern
enquiry [ɪn'kwaɪəri]	Anfrage
to ensure [ɪn'ʃʊə]	sicherstellen, gewährleisten
environmentally friendly [ɪnˌvaɪrənˌmentəli 'frendli]	umweltfreundlich
to equip [ɪ'kwɪp]	ausstatten
equipment [ɪ'kwɪpmənt]	Geräte, Ausstattung, Ausrüstung
to estimate ['estɪmeɪt]	schätzen, abschätzen
evenly ['i:vnli]	gleichmäßig
to exceed [ɪk'si:d]	überschreiten
exhibitor [ɪg'zɪbɪtə]	Aussteller
expenditures [ɪk'spendɪtʃəz]	Ausgaben
expertise [ˌekspɜ:'ti:z]	(Fach-)Kompetenz, Sachkenntnis
explosive [ɪk'spləʊsɪv]	explosionsgefährlich, explosiv
export licence ['ekspɔ:t laɪsns]	Ausfuhrgenehmigung, Exportlizenz
extensive [ɪk'stensɪv]	umfassend, umfangreich

F

factory gate ['fæktəri geɪt]	Fabriktor
factory gate pricing [fæktəri ˌgeɪt 'praɪsɪŋ]	Ab-Werk-Preis (ohne Transportkosten)
feature ['fi:tʃə]	Eigenschaft, Besonderheit
fierce [fɪəs]	(Wettbewerb:) hart
fitted with sth ['fɪtɪd wɪð]	mit etw versehen
flat-rack container [ˌflæt ræk kən'teɪnə]	Flachgestellcontainer
fleet [fli:t]	Flotte
fleet of vehicles [ˌfli:t əv 'vi:əklz]	Fahrzeugflotte
fluctuation [ˌflʌktʃu'eɪʃn]	Schwankung
fog [fɒg]	Nebel
foodstuffs ['fu:dstʌfs]	Lebensmittel
forecast ['fɔ:kɑ:st]	Schätzung, Prognose
foreign trade [ˌfɒrən 'treɪd]	Außenhandel
fork-lift truck [ˌfɔ:klɪft 'trʌk]	Gabelstapler
forwarding ['fɔ:wədɪŋ]	Versand, Transport
forwarding agent ['fɔ:wədɪŋ eɪdʒənt]	Spedition
fragile ['frædʒaɪl]	zerbrechlich
frame [freɪm]	Rahmen, Gestell
freight [freɪt]	Fracht
freight forwarder ['freɪt fɔ:wədə]	Spediteur
freight invoice ['freɪt ɪnvɔɪs]	Frachtrechnung
fuel ['fju:əl]	Brennstoff, Treibstoff
fulfilment [fʊl'fɪlmənt]	Auftragsabwicklung

G

gatehouse ['geɪthaʊs]	Pforte, Werkstor
general purpose [ˌdʒenrəl 'pɜ:pəs]	Allzweck-
to generate ['dʒenəreɪt]	erzeugen, generieren, erwirtschaften
to get back to sb [ˌget 'bæk tə]	sich wieder bei jdm melden
to get on to sth [ˌget 'ɒn tə]	sich um etw kümmern
goods [gʊdz]	Waren, Güter
grain [greɪn]	Getreide
granite ['grænɪt]	Granit
to grant [grɑ:nt]	gewähren, bewilligen
gantry crane ['gæntri kreɪn]	Containerbrücke
gross [grəʊs]	brutto
gross weight [ˌgrəʊs 'weɪt]	Bruttogewicht
ground space [ˌgraʊnd 'speɪs]	Lagerfläche
growth [grəʊθ]	Wachstum
growth rate ['grəʊθ reɪt]	Wachstumsrate

H

to hand over [ˌhænd 'əʊvə]	übergeben
hand pallet-truck [hænd ˌpælət 'trʌk]	(Handgabel-)Hubwagen
to handle ['hændl]	umschlagen, befördern, bearbeiten, erledigen
handling ['hændlɪŋ]	Handhabung, Umschlag, Beförderung, Erledigung
handling damage ['hændlɪŋ dæmɪdʒ]	Transportschaden
handy ['hændi]	praktisch
harbour ['hɑ:bə]	Hafen
harbour, maritime ~ [ˌmærɪtaɪm 'hɑ:bə]	Seehafen
harmful ['hɑ:mfl]	schädlich
harmonized tariff system (HTS) [ˌhɑ:mənaɪzd 'tærɪf sɪstəm]	einheitliches Tarifsystem für Importe
haulage contractor [ˌhɔ:lɪdʒ kən'træktə]	(Straßen-)Spediteur
haulier ['hɔ:lɪə]	(Straßen-)Spediteur
hazardous ['hæzədəs]	gefährlich, gefahrvoll
hazardous material [ˌhæzədəs mə'tɪərɪəl]	Gefahrstoff, Gefahrgut
heavyweight cargo [ˌheviweɪt 'kɑ:gəʊ]	Schwerlast
HGV driving ban [ˌeɪtʃ dʒi: ˌvi: 'draɪvɪŋ bæn]	LKW-Fahrverbot
high-racking storage [haɪ ˌrækɪŋ 'stɔ:rɪdʒ]	Hochregallager
to hire sb ['haɪə]	jdn einstellen
hold-up ['həʊldʌp]	Verzögerung
hook [hʊk]	Haken
host [həʊst]	Gastgeber/in, Veranstalter/in

I

impact ['ɪmpækt]	Auswirkung, Konsequenz
import ban ['ɪmpɔ:t bæn]	Einfuhrverbot
importance [ɪm'pɔ:tns]	Bedeutung, Wichtigkeit
impressive [ɪm'presɪv]	beeindruckend
inconvenience [ˌɪnkən'vi:nɪəns]	Unannehmlichkeit, Umstände
increase ['ɪŋkri:s]	Zunahme, Steigerung
to increase [ɪn'kri:s]	steigern
industrial boiler [ɪnˌdʌstrɪəl 'bɔɪlə]	Industriekessel
industry ['ɪndəstri]	Branche, Industrie
infrequent [ɪn'fri:kwənt]	selten
insolvency [ɪn'sɒlvənsi]	Insolvenz
to instruct [ɪn'strʌkt]	unterrichten, unterweisen
instruction [ɪn'strʌkʃn]	Anweisung, Vorschrift
insurance [ɪn'ʃʊərəns]	Versicherung
insurance policy [ɪn'ʃʊərəns pɒləsi]	Versicherungspolice
to insure [ɪn'ʃʊə]	versichern
intermediate bulk container (IBC) [ɪntəˌmi:dɪət ˌbʌlk kən'teɪnə]	Schüttgutzwischenbehälter
International Standards Organization (ISO) [ɪntəˌnæʃnəl 'stændədz ɔ:gənaɪzeɪʃn]	Internationale Organisation für Normung (ISO)
inventory ['ɪnvəntri]	(Lager-)Bestand
inventory management ['ɪnvəntri mænɪdʒmənt]	Bestandsführung
invoice ['ɪnvɔɪs]	Rechnung
invoice, commercial ~ [kəˌmɜ:ʃl 'ɪnvɔɪs]	Handelsrechnung, Warenrechnung
invoice, consular ~ [ˌkɒnsjələ 'ɪnvɔɪs]	Konsulatsrechnung, -faktura
invoice, customs ~ ['kʌstəmz ɪnvɔɪs]	Zollfaktura, Zollrechnung
invoice, freight ~ ['freɪt ɪnvɔɪs]	Frachtrechnung

invoice, pro forma ~ [ˌprəʊ ˈfɔːmə ˈɪnvɔɪs]	Proformarechnung	
to **involve** [ɪnˈvɒlv]	mit sich bringen, beteiligen	
irrevocable letter of credit [ɪˌrevəkəbl ˌletər əv ˈkredɪt]	unwiderrufliches Dokumentenakkreditiv	
issue [ˈɪʃuː]	Frage, Problem, Ausgabe	
to **issue** [ˈɪʃuː]	ausgeben, erstellen, (Anweisung) erteilen	
item [ˈaɪtəm]	Artikel, Ware	

J

job specification [ˈdʒɒb spesɪfɪkeɪʃn]	Stellenbeschreibung

K

to **keep track of sth** [ˌkiːp ˈtræk əv]	etw (eine Sendung) verfolgen
kitting [ˈkɪtɪŋ]	Konfektionierung, Montage

L

label [ˈleɪbl]	Etikett, Aufkleber
labelling [ˈleɪblɪŋ]	Etikettieren
lading, bill of ~ [ˌbɪl əv ˈleɪdɪŋ]	Schiffsfrachtbrief
large goods vehicle (LGV) [ˌlɑːdʒ ˌɡʊdz ˈviːəkl]	Lastkraftwagen (über 3,5 t)
large-volume shipment [ˌlɑːdʒ ˌvɒljuːm ˈʃɪpmənt]	großvolumige Ladung
to **lash** [læʃ]	festzurren
lashing [ˈlæʃɪŋ]	Verschnüren, Befestigung
lashing device [ˈlæʃɪŋ dɪvaɪs]	Zurrvorrichtung
launch [lɔːntʃ]	Start, Markteinführung
lead time [ˈliːd taɪm]	Durchlaufzeit, Vorlaufzeit
letter of credit [ˌletər əv ˈkredɪt]	Akkreditiv
letter of credit, irrevocable ~ [ɪˌrevəkəbl ˌletər əv ˈkredɪt]	unwiderrufliches Akkreditiv
to **liaise with** [liˈeɪz wɪð]	zusammenarbeiten mit
lid [lɪd]	Deckel
liner bag [ˈlaɪnə bæɡ]	Containerauskleidung, Schutzplane
liquid [ˈlɪkwɪd]	Flüssigkeit
literature fulfilment [ˈlɪtrətʃə fʊlfɪlmənt]	(komplette) Informations- und Dokumentationsabwicklung
load [ləʊd]	Ladung
loading capacity [ˈləʊdɪŋ kəpæsəti]	Ladekapazität, Tragkraft, Fassungsvermögen
loading time [ˈləʊdɪŋ taɪm]	Ladezeit
lorry [ˈlɒri]	Lastwagen, Lkw
lump sum [ˌlʌmp ˈsʌm]	Pauschalbetrag, Geldbetrag

M

machinery [məˈʃiːnəri]	Maschinen
to **maintain** [meɪnˈteɪn]	instandhalten, unterhalten, aufrechterhalten, warten
maintenance [ˈmeɪntənəns]	Instandhaltung
manual [ˈmænjuəl]	Handbuch, Anleitung
manufacturer [ˌmænjuˈfæktʃərə]	Hersteller, Fabrikant, Produzent
marble [ˈmɑːbl]	Marmor
maritime harbour [ˌmærɪtaɪm ˈhɑːbə]	Seehafen
to **mark** [mɑːk]	kennzeichnen
marking [ˈmɑːkɪŋ]	Kennzeichnung
marshalling [ˈmɑːʃlɪŋ]	Bereitstellung
material flow [məˈtɪəriəl fləʊ]	Materialfluss
means of carriage [ˌmiːnz əv ˈkærɪdʒ]	Transportmittel
measure [ˈmeʒə]	Maß; Maßnahme
to **measure** [ˈmeʒə]	messen
measurement [ˈmeʒəmənt]	Maß, Abmessung
to **meet requirements** [ˌmiːt rɪˈkwaɪəmənts]	Anforderungen erfüllen
mobile shelving [ˌməʊbaɪl ˈʃelvɪŋ]	Verschieberegal
mode [məʊd]	Art, Verfahren, Methode
mode of transport [ˌməʊd əv ˈtrænspɔːt]	Beförderungsart, Verkehrsträger
moisture [ˈmɔɪstʃə]	Feuchtigkeit
to **monitor** [ˈmɒnɪtə]	überwachen, kontrollieren
to **mount** [maʊnt]	montieren, befestigen, aufbauen
movement [ˈmuːvmənt]	Beförderung
multimodal [ˌmʌltiˈməʊdl]	multimodal

N

to **negotiate** [nɪˈɡəʊʃieɪt]	verhandeln
negotiation [nɪˌɡəʊʃiˈeɪʃn]	Verhandlung
net [net]	netto
non-hazardous [ˌnɒn ˈhæzədəs]	ungefährlich
non-payment [ˌnɒnˈpeɪmənt]	Zahlungsverweigerung, Nichtzahlung
non-vessel operating common carrier (NVOCC) [nɒn ˌvesl ˌɒpəreɪtɪŋ ˌkɒmən ˈkæriə]	Schiffsbuchender Verfrachter, Reeder ohne Schiff

O

to **obtain** [əbˈteɪn]	erhalten
on behalf of [ɒn bɪˈhɑːf əv]	im Auftrag von
open account [ˌəʊpən əˈkaʊnt]	Kontokorrent, gegen Rechnung
open account facilities [ˌəʊpən əˌkaʊnt fəˈsɪlətiz]	offenes Zahlungsziel, Zahlung gegen Rechnung
open-top container [ˌəʊpən tɒp kənˈteɪnə]	Open-Top-Container
operation [ˌɒpəˈreɪʃn]	Aktivität, Unternehmen, Arbeitsvorgang
operational costs [ˌɒpəˌreɪʃnl ˈkɒsts]	Betriebskosten
order [ˈɔːdə]	Auftrag, Bestellung
order picking [ˈɔːdə pɪkɪŋ]	Kommissionieren
origin [ˈɒrɪdʒɪn]	Herkunft(sort)
out of stock [ˌaʊt əv ˈstɒk]	nicht vorrätig, nicht am Lager
outdated [ˌaʊtˈdeɪtɪd]	veraltet
outlet [ˈaʊtlet]	Verkaufsstelle
output [ˈaʊtpʊt]	Produktion
to **outsource** [ˈaʊtsɔːs]	auslagern
to **overcome** [ˌəʊvəˈkʌm]	überwinden, bewältigen
overhanging [ˈəʊvəhæŋɪŋ]	überstehend
to **overload** [ˌəʊvəˈləʊd]	überladen, überlasten
overseas [ˌəʊvəˈsiːz]	im/ins Ausland
to **oversee** [ˌəʊvəˈsiː]	beaufsichtigen, überwachen
to **overspend** [ˌəʊvəˈspend]	(Etat) überziehen
overwidth [ˈəʊvəwɪdθ]	Überbreite

P

pace [peɪs]	Tempo
package [ˈpækɪdʒ]	Verpackung
packaging [ˈpækɪdʒɪŋ]	Verpackung(smaterial)
packing [ˈpækɪŋ]	verpacken
packing list [ˈpækɪŋ lɪst]	Packliste, Versandliste
packing location [ˈpækɪŋ ləʊkeɪʃn]	Verpackungsort (am Fließband)
packing material [ˌpækɪŋ məˈtɪəriəl]	Verpackungsmaterial, Packmaterial
pallet [ˈpælət]	Palette
pallet racking [ˈpælət rækɪŋ]	Palettenregal
pallet, adjustable ~ racking (APR) [əˌdʒʌstəl ˈpælət rækɪŋ]	verstellbares Palettenregalsystem
pallet, hand ~-truck [hænd ˌpælət ˈtrʌk]	(Handgabel-)Hubwagen
pallet, roll-cage ~ [ˌrəʊl keɪdʒ ˈpælət]	Rollcontainer
panel [ˈpænl]	Platte
parcel [ˈpɑːsl]	Expressgut, Paket
part load [ˈpɑːt ləʊd]	Teilladung, Teilpartie
partial [ˈpɑːʃl]	Teil-
partial delivery [ˌpɑːʃl dɪˈlɪvəri]	Teillieferung
to **pay up front** [peɪ ˌʌp ˈfrʌnt]	im Voraus bezahlen
payload [ˈpeɪləʊd]	Zuladung
perishables [ˈperɪʃəblz]	verderbliche Waren
picking [ˈpɪkɪŋ]	Kommissionieren
pick-up [ˈpɪkʌp]	Abholung
piggyback [ˈpɪɡibæk]	Huckepack
to **pile** [paɪl]	stapeln
pipe [paɪp]	Röhre
to **place an order** [ˌpleɪs ən ˈɔːdə]	einen Auftrag erteilen
plant [plɑːnt]	Fabrik
plug, electric ~ [ɪˌlektrɪk ˈplʌɡ]	Steckdose, Elektroanschluss
point of origin [ˌpɔɪnt əv ˈɒrɪdʒɪn]	Herkunftsort

A–Z wordlist | 91

point of sale [ˌpɔɪnt əf 'seɪl]	Verkaufsstelle
political unrest [pəˌlɪtɪkl ʌn'rest]	politische Unruhen
polybagging ['pɒlibægɪŋ]	Folienverpackung
to predict [prɪ'dɪkt]	voraussagen, vorhersagen
premises ['premɪsɪz]	Gelände
pricing ['praɪsɪŋ]	Preisgestaltung
pro forma invoice [ˌprəʊ 'fɔːmə ɪnvɔɪs]	Proformarechnung
proactive, to be ~ [bi ˌprəʊ'æktɪv]	Eigeninitiative zeigen
to process ['prəʊses]	verarbeiten, bearbeiten
processing ['prəʊsesɪŋ]	Bearbeitung
procurement [prə'kjʊəmənt]	Beschaffung
produce ['prɒdjuːs]	landwirtschaftliche Erzeugnisse
product range ['prɒdʌkt reɪndʒ]	Produktpalette, Angebot
production plant [prə'dʌkʃn plɑːnt]	Produktionsstätte, Fabrik
profit margin ['prɒfɪt mɑːdʒɪn]	Gewinnspanne
protruding [prə'truːdɪŋ]	vorstehend, überstehend
to provide [prə'vaɪd]	liefern, zur Verfügung stellen, bieten
provider [prə'vaɪdə]	Anbieter, Dienstleister
purchase ['pɜːtʃəs]	Kauf
to purchase ['pɜːtʃəs]	kaufen, einkaufen
purchasing (department) ['pɜːtʃəsɪŋ dɪpɑːtmənt]	Einkauf(sabteilung)
purchasing manager ['pɜːtʃəsɪŋ mænɪdʒə]	Einkaufsleiter
put-away instruction [ˌpʊt ə'weɪ ɪnstrʌkʃn]	Einlagerungsanweisung

Q

quantity ['kwɒntəti]	Menge
quantity discount ['kwɒntəti dɪskaʊnt]	Mengenrabatt
quotation [kwəʊ'teɪʃn]	Angebot, Kostenvoranschlag
to quote for sth ['kwəʊt fə]	einen Kostenvoranschlag/ein Angebot für etw machen
to quote a price [ˌkwəʊt ə 'praɪs]	einen Preis anbieten/ansetzen

R

radio-frequency identification (RFID) [ˌreɪdiəʊ ˌfriːkwənsi aɪdentɪfɪ'keɪʃn]	Funkerkennung
rail [reɪl]	(Eisenbahn-)Schiene
rail-mounted ['reɪl maʊntɪd]	auf Schienen montiert
railway track ['reɪlweɪ træk]	(Eisenbahn-)Gleis
rate [reɪt]	Gebühr, Satz, Steuer, Frachtrate
reach stacker ['riːtʃ stækə]	Greifstapler
real time [ˌrɪəl 'taɪm]	Echtzeit
receipt [rɪ'siːt]	Empfang, Erhalt, Quittung, Empfangsbestätigung
receipt of order [rɪˌsiːt əv 'ɔːdə]	Auftragseingang
receiving [rɪ'siːvɪŋ]	Wareneingang
records ['rekɔːdz]	Daten, Unterlagen
reefer ['riːfə]	Kühlcontainer
refrigerated container [rɪˌfrɪdʒəreɪtɪd kən'teɪnə]	Kühlcontainer
regulations [ˌregju'leɪʃnz]	Vorschriften
to reject [rɪ'dʒekt]	zurückweisen, ablehnen
rejected, to be [bi rɪ'dʒektɪd]	zurückweisen werden
reliable [rɪ'laɪəbl]	zuverlässig
reliance on sth [rɪ'laɪəns ɒn]	Abhängigkeit von etw
to remit [rɪ'mɪt]	(Geld) zahlen, überweisen
replacement [rɪ'pleɪsmənt]	Ersatz, Austausch
replenishment [rɪ'plenɪʃmənt]	Lagerauffüllung, Auffüllen
replenishment, continuous ~ (CRP) [kənˌtɪnjuəs rɪ'plenɪʃmənt]	kontinuierliche Bestandsauffüllung
to report [rɪ'pɔːt]	berichten, sich melden
request [rɪ'kwest]	Wunsch, Bitte, Anfrage
requirement [rɪ'kwaɪəmənt]	Wunsch, Anforderung, Bedingung
reserve storage [rɪˌzɜːv 'stɔːrɪdʒ]	Reservelager
responsibility [rɪˌspɒnsə'bɪləti]	Zuständigkeit, Aufgabenbereich
responsible, to be ~ for sth [bi rɪ'spɒnsəbl fə]	für etw zuständig/verantwortlich sein
retail ['riːteɪl]	Einzelhandel
retail price [ˌriːteɪl 'praɪs]	Einzelhandelspreis, Endverkaufspreis
retrieval [rɪ'triːvl]	(Lager:) Entnahme
to retrieve [rɪ'triːv]	wiederfinden
return [rɪ'tɜːn]	Retoure
returns processing [rɪˌtɜːn 'prəʊsesɪŋ]	Retourenbearbeitung
reverse logistics [rɪˌvɜːs lə'dʒɪstɪks]	Rücklieferungslogistik, Rückwärtslogistik
to review [rɪ'vjuː]	überprüfen
rigid ['rɪdʒɪd]	starr, fest
river barge ['rɪvə bɑːdʒ]	Lastkahn (für die Binnenschifffahrt)
road-rail trailer [ˌrəʊd 'reɪl treɪlə]	Straßen-Schienen-Sattelauflieger
roll-cage pallet [ˌrəʊl keɪdʒ 'pælət]	Rollcontainer
roof panel [ˌruːf 'pænl]	Dachplatte

S

sailing ['seɪlɪŋ]	Überfahrt, Passage, Abfahrt
sailing time ['seɪlɪŋ taɪm]	Abfahrtszeit
sales [seɪlz]	Vertrieb, Verkauf
scales [skeɪlz]	Waage
schedule ['ʃedjuːl]	Plan
schedule, on ~ [ɒn 'ʃedjuːl]	pünktlich
to schedule ['ʃedjuːl]	planen, vorsehen, festlegen
scheduled ['ʃedjuːld]	planmäßig, vorgesehen, geplant
sea freight ['siː freɪt]	Seefracht
seafood ['siːfuːd]	Meeresfrüchte
seagoing vessel [ˌsiːgəʊɪŋ 'vesl]	Hochseeschiff
to seal [siːl]	verschließen, versiegeln
seasonal ['siːznəl]	saisonal
secure [sɪ'kjʊə]	sicher
to secure [sɪ'kjʊə]	sichern
selling profile ['selɪŋ prəʊfaɪl]	Produktkatalog
services ['sɜːvɪsɪz]	Dienstleistungen
settlement ['setlmənt]	(Geldgeschäft:) Zahlung, Saldierung, Begleichung
shelving, mobile ~ [ˌməʊbaɪl 'ʃelvɪŋ]	Verschieberegal
shift [ʃɪft]	Verlagerung, Verschiebung, Veränderung
shipment ['ʃɪpmənt]	Beförderung, Transport, Versand; Sendung, Ladung
shipper ['ʃɪpə]	Versender, Absender, Verlader
shipping ['ʃɪpɪŋ]	Transport, Versand
shipping label ['ʃɪpɪŋ leɪbl]	Versandschein, Versandetikett
shipping line ['ʃɪpɪŋ laɪn]	Reederei, Schifffahrtsgesellschaft
shipping order ['ʃɪpɪŋ ɔːdə]	Versandauftrag
shipping rate ['ʃɪpɪŋ reɪt]	Transport-, Versandkosten, Frachtsatz
short notice, at ~ [ət ˌʃɔːt 'nəʊtɪs]	kurzfristig
shortage ['ʃɔːtɪdʒ]	Engpass
shrink-wrapping ['ʃrɪŋk ræpɪŋ]	Schrumpffolienverpackung
shuffling system ['ʃʌflɪŋ sɪstəm]	Sortieranlage (Post)
single wagon [ˌsɪŋgl 'wægən]	Einzelwagen, -waggon
slat [slæt]	Holzlatte
solvent ['sɒlvənt]	zahlungsfähig, liquide, solvent
sophisticated [sə'fɪstɪkeɪtɪd]	hochentwickelt
to sort out [ˌsɔːt 'aʊt]	lösen, klären
sortation [sɔː'teɪʃn]	Sortierung
to source [sɔːs]	beziehen, beschaffen
sourcing ['sɔːsɪŋ]	Bezug, Beschaffung
space [speɪs]	Raum, Frachtraum, Fläche
to specify ['spesɪfaɪ]	(genau) angeben
spout [spaʊt]	Schütte, Auslaufrohr
spreader beam ['spredə biːm]	Traverse

to stack [stæk]	stapeln	
stackable ['stækəbl]	stapelbar	
staff [stɑːf]	Personal	
stakeholder ['steɪkhəʊldə]	Beteiligte/r	
staple ['steɪpl]	Heftklammer	
to state [steɪt]	nennen, angeben	
statement ['steɪtmənt]	Übersicht, Aufstellung, (Konto-)Auszug	
steel [stiːl]	Stahl	
stock [stɒk]	(Waren-, Lager-)Bestand	
stock control ['stɒk kəntrəʊl]	Lagerkontrolle, Bestandsüberwachung	
stock, out of ~ [ˌaʊt əv 'stɒk]	nicht vorrätig, nicht am Lager	
to stock [stɒk]	lagern, bevorraten	
storage ['stɔːrɪdʒ]	Lagerung	
store [stɔː]	Lager, Magazin; Vorrat	
store supervisor ['stɔː suːpəvaɪzə]	Lagermeister/in	
to store [stɔː]	lagern	
to straddle ['strædl]	überspannen, übergreifen	
straddle carrier ['strædl kæriə]	fahrbare Containerbrücke, Portalhubwagen	
to strap [stræp]	festschnallen, festzurren	
stretch-wrapping ['stretʃ ræpɪŋ]	Dehnfolienumwicklung, -verpackung	
sturdy ['stɜːdi]	robust, stabil	
subject, to be ~ to sth [bɪ 'sʌbdʒɪkt tə]	einer Sache unterliegen	
suitable ['suːtəbl]	geeignet	
to supervise ['suːpəvaɪz]	überwachen, beaufsichtigen	
supplier [sə'plaɪə]	Lieferant, Zulieferer	
supplies [sə'plaɪz]	Ausstattung, Betriebsstoffe	
supply [sə'plaɪ]	Lieferung, Versorgung, Bereitstellung	
supply chain [sə'plaɪ tʃeɪn]	Lieferkette	
to supply [sə'plaɪ]	liefern, zur Verfügung stellen	
support [sə'pɔːt]	Unterstützung	
to support [sə'pɔːt]	unterstützen	
surface ['sɜːfɪs]	Oberfläche	
suspend [sə'spend]	aussetzen, anhalten	
sustainable [sə'steɪnəbl]	nachhaltig	
swap-body ['swɒpbɒdi]	Wechselbrücke, Wechselaufbau	

T

tag [tæg]	Indentifikationsmarke	
tailor-made [ˌteɪlə'meɪd]	maßgeschneidert	
to take out insurance [teɪk ˌaʊt ɪn'ʃʊərəns]	eine Versicherung abschließen	
tanktainer [ˌtæŋk'teɪnə]	Tanktainer	
tare weight [ˌteə 'weɪt]	Leergewicht, Tara	
tariff ['tærɪf]	Tarif, *insbes.* Zolltarif	
tariff, harmonized ~ system (HTS) [ˌhɑːmənaɪzd 'tærɪf sɪstəm]	einheitliches Tarifsystem für Importe	
tarpaulin [tɑː'pɔːlɪn]	Plane, Verdeck	
technique [tek'niːk]	Methode, Technik	
tender ['tendə]	Angebot	
terms and conditions [ˌtɜːmz ənd kən'dɪʃnz]	Geschäftsbedingungen, Konditionen	
third-party logistics [θɜːd ˌpɑːti lə'dʒɪstɪks]	Logistikdienstleistungen, Logistikdienstleister	
third-party provider [θɜːd ˌpɑːti prə'vaɪdə]	Drittanbieter	
This side up [θɪs ˌsaɪd 'ʌp]	(Paket:) Hier oben	
tightly bound [ˌtaɪtli 'baʊnd]	fest verschnürt	
timber ['tɪmbə]	(Bau-, Nutz-)Holz	
timber floor [ˌtɪmbə 'flɔː]	Holzboden	
tote bin ['təʊt bɪn]	Transportbehälter	
toxic ['tɒksɪk]	giftig	
track, to keep ~ of sth [ˌkiːp 'træk əv]	etw *(eine Sendung)* verfolgen	
to track sth [træk]	*(eine Sendung)* verfolgen	
tracking and tracing [ˌtrækɪŋ ən 'treɪsɪŋ]	Verfolgung und Ortung *(von Sendungen)*	
trade [treɪd]	Handel	
trade discount ['treɪd dɪskaʊnt]	Handelsrabatt	
trailer ['treɪlə]	(Sattel-)Anhänger, Auflieger	
train, block ~ ['blɒk treɪn]	Ganzzug, Blockzug	
to train sb [treɪn]	jdn schulen, ausbilden	
transfer ['trænsfɜː]	Überweisung	
to transfer [træns'fɜː]	*(Informationen)* übermitteln, *(Geld)* überweisen	
transit, in ~ [ɪn 'trænzɪt]	unterwegs, während des Transports	
transshipment [træns'ʃɪpmənt]	Frachtumschlag, Umladung	
trillion ['trɪljən]	Billion	
trolley ['trɒli]	Sackkarre	

U

unloading bay [ʌn'ləʊdɪŋ beɪ]	Entladeplatz, Entladebucht	
unrest [ʌn'rest]	Unruhen	
up front, to pay ~ [peɪ ˌʌp 'frʌnt]	im Voraus bezahlen	
upset, to be [bɪ ʌp'set]	verärgert/bestürzt sein	
urban area [ˌɜːbən 'eəriə]	Ballungsraum	
urgent ['ɜːdʒənt]	dringend, eilig	

V

value ['væljuː]	Wert	
value-added [ˌvæljuː 'ædɪd]	Mehrwert-	
value-added services [ˌvæljuː ˌædɪd 'sɜːvɪsɪz]	Mehrwertleistungen	
vehicle ['viːəkl]	Fahrzeug	
vehicle, large goods ~ (LGV) [lɑːdʒ ˌgʊdz 'viːəkl]	Lastkraftwagen *(über 3,5 t)*	
vendor ['vendə]	Verkäufer, Anbieter, Lieferant	

W

wagon ['wægən]	(Eisenbahn-)Waggon	
wagon, single ~ [ˌsɪŋgl 'wægən]	Einzelwagen/-waggon	
warehouse management ['weəhaʊs mænɪdʒmənt]	Lagerverwaltung	
warehouse tracking ['weəhaʊs trækɪŋ]	Lagerplatzbestimmung	
warehousing ['weəhaʊzɪŋ]	Lagerung, Lagerhaltung, Lagerwesen	
waterway ['wɔːtəweɪ]	Wasserstraße	
waybill ['weɪbɪl]	Frachtbrief, Warenbegleitschein	
weight [weɪt]	Gewicht	
wholesaler ['həʊlseɪlə]	Großhändler/in	
to withstand sth [wɪð'stænd]	etw aushalten	
to wrap [ræp]	umwickeln, einwickeln	
wrapping, shrink-~ ['ʃrɪŋk ræpɪŋ]	Schrumpffolienumwicklung, -verpackung	
wrapping, stretch-~ ['stretʃ ræpɪŋ]	Dehnfolienumwicklung, -verpackung	

Y

yard [jɑːd]	Hof, Gelände	

Useful phrases

TALKING ABOUT YOUR JOB

What do you do?
What's your line of work?
I work for a major shipping company.
I work in the regional depot.
I'm responsible for …
In my job I have to …
My job involves …
I often …
I work for an international logistics company.
He usually spends a lot of time with his customers.
Do you ship goods to Asia?
He doesn't work in the European office.

SELLING YOUR COMPANY'S SERVICES

We can offer you a wide range of …
We can provide (you with) customized/tailor-made logistics solutions for …
We spezialize in …
As a specialist for/in … we can …
With our many years of experience …
We have experience and expertise in providing …
Our team will be happy to handle …/assist you with …
With our dedicated team of logistics experts we can …
The price request tool allows you to obtain prices for shipments.
E-Shipping helps you prepare/print/track/select … online.
To … , (just) sign up/register for/log on to …
For price requests, please use …
To access shipment details, click …

DESCRIBING PROCESSES

The goods are delivered to a depot.
The order is generated by the computer.
Problems are quickly identified.
Information is transferred to the warehouse.
The forks can be raised by a simple pump action.
This system must be fitted with detectors.
After the goods have been checked, they go into backup storage.
The unloading has been completed.

ASKING FOR AND GIVING OPINIONS

What do you think?
How do you feel about that?
What are your thoughts on that?
Do you agree?
I suggest that we …
In my opinion we should …
Perhaps we should …
Why don't we …
That's a good idea.
That sounds good.
I agree.
That's right.

REQUESTING A QUOTATION

We/I need a quotation for a shipment to …
Please quote for (the supply/transport of) …
Please send us a quotation for …
Please quote your lowest price for …
Your quotation should include detailed information on freight and insurance rates, delivery terms, delivery date, and terms of payment.

GIVING A QUOTATION

Please find attached our quotation for …
We are pleased to quote as follows.
We can quote you a gross/net price of …
The prices quoted above include …
We can offer you a price of … per …
We can offer you 10 % off the retail price.
We allow a 2 % cash discount for payment within 30 days.
Our prices are subject to a 25 % trade discount off net price.
We grant a trade/quantity/cash discount of … % on our list prices.
If your order exceeds 2,000 items, we can offer you a further 10 % discount.
Delivery can be effected immediately after receipt of order.
As requested, we will deliver on pallets to …
We would be able to deliver within ten days of receipt of order.

MAKING COMPARISONS

Transport by sea is cheaper than transport by air.
Steel is heavier than paper.
Shipping goods by road is more expensive than shipping them by rail.
Some transport modes are more reliable than others.
Our rates are better than theirs.
Their service is worse than ours.
This shipment will travel further than the last one.

MAKING ENQUIRIES

I'd like to ask/enquire about …
I'm calling about …
I'm writing about/with regard to …
Could you tell me how much/many/long/often …?

ADVISING THE CUSTOMER

For this consignment I would recommend/suggest using air transport.
I recommend/suggest that you ship the goods by road.
We/You should also consider air transport for …
That depends on your specific requirements.
Another option would be to …
Of course it would also be possible to … (instead).
Alternatively, you/we could …

Useful phrases

TALKING ABOUT DIMENSIONS AND WEIGHT

Our consignment is 3 by 2 by 2.5 metres.
This box measures 2 by 1.5 by 2.5 metres.
Its measurements are 20 by 85 by 60 centimetres.
The empty container weighs 5,000 kg.
The net/tare/gross weight of the container is … kg/tons.
The container's maximum payload is …
The box is 40 cm high/long/wide/deep.
Its/the height/length/width/depth is 40 cm.

TALKING ABOUT PROBLEMS

I'm afraid there is a problem with customs clearance.
I'm sorry, but there will be a delivery delay.
The delay was caused by a rail strike in Italy.
The consignment has to be repacked because the carton is damaged.
There was a delay because of bad weather.
There was a delay because the weather was bad.
Although the load wasn't secured properly, it arrived intact.
The load wasn't secured properly, but it arrived intact.
In spite of the strike, the consignment arrived on time.
The result was that the goods didn't leave the warehouse until Friday.
As a result, the shipment arrived two hours late.
There's fog at the airport so the flight hasn't taken off yet.

ADVISING CUSTOMERS OF SHIPMENT

We are pleased to inform you that Order N° 30-12 has been dispatched by truck today.
Order No 30-12 has been dispatched by flight BA0237A today.
We are pleased to advise that your order N° 23/1346 was shipped on board the vessel Ocean Line.
The consignment is due to arrive in Sydney on 25th August.
The above order has been handed over to our forwarding agents today.
The consignment will be delivered to your warehouse in Brussels.

TALKING ABOUT ADVANTAGES AND POSSIBLE IMPROVEMENTS

One great advantage is …
The most interesting feature is …
It would help us reduce/increase/improve/optimize …
Another major advantage is/would be …
It would also guarantee/ensure …

DESCRIBING THE STEPS OF A PROCESS

First(ly)/First of all …
The first step/stage (of the process) is …
Second(ly) …
Then …
After that …
The next step/stage is …
Following that …
Finally …
The last step is …
Once/After X has happened …

DEALING WITH COMPLAINTS

Thank you for informing us about an error in our December statement. (formal)
Thanks very much for pointing out the mistake.
I understand there is a confusion in addresses/delivery dates.
We are looking into this matter and will contact you again later today. (formal)
I will get in touch with the forwarding agent at once.
I'll take care of this straight away.
I'll get on to that now.
I'll see to this immediately.
I'll get back to you on that as soon as possible.
We would like to apologize for the inconvenience. (formal)
We very much regret this misunderstanding. (formal)
I'm very sorry about that.
Let me apologize for this delay/mistake/error (once again).
The consignment must be delivered by Friday.
The logistics manager will be away until Friday.

DEALING WITH PAYMENT

Please find attached our pro forma invoice for order N° 45-09-23.
We enclose a copy of your invoice. The original will be sent to you together with the documents on settlement of our draft.
We have instructed our bank today to transfer/remit the amount of £6,320 to your account with Royal Bank of Scotland.
Please find enclosed a cheque for $745.55 in payment of your invoice N° 2/08/2457.
We enclose our draft for $23,840 drawn on Pacific Bank, Seattle. Could you please acknowledge receipt?
Thank you for your credit transfer for 4,500 in payment of our July statement.
Our bank has advised us today that your transfer for invoice N° FR 1235 has been credited to our account.
We have received your draft for invoice N° 12349. Thank you for sending it so promptly.

DEALING WITH MISTAKES

It seems/appears that a mistake has been made with regard to the customs invoice.
There seems to be a discrepancy between the items listed on your June statement and the goods delivered.
When checking your statement, we noted that invoice TX 274 has been debited twice.
We are returning your invoice as the 2% discount has not been deducted from the total amount.
Could you please let us have a corrected/an amended invoice by return?
Could you make sure that weight and dimensions of the items are specified on the commercial invoice?

Glossary of acronyms and abbreviations

APR	adjustable pallet racking
AS/RS	automated storage and retrieval system
AWB	air waybill
B/E	bill of exchange
B/L	bill of lading
BTN	Brussels tariff number
CAD	cash against documents
CM	category management
CO	certificate of origin
COD	cash on delivery
CRP	continuous replenishment
D/P	documents against payment
DC	distribution centre
DSD	direct store delivery
EDI	electronic data interchange
ETA	estimated time of arrival
ETS	estimated time of sailing
FCL	full container load
GPC	general purpose container
GPS	global positioning system
HGV	heavy goods vehicle
HTS	harmonized tariff system
IATA	International Air Transport Association
IBC	intermediate bulk container
IMO	international money order
ISO	International Standards Organization
JIT	just-in-time
LC	letter of credit
LCL	less than container load
LGV	large goods vehicle
NVOCC	non-vessel operating common carrier
POD	proof of delivery
QR	quick response
RFID	radio frequency identification
RMS	resource management system
RORO	roll-on/roll-off ferry
SCM	supply chain management
SMS	short message service
3PL	third-party logistics
VAL	value-added logistics
VAS	value-added services
VMI	vendor-managed inventory
WMS	warehouse management system

Weights and measures conversion chart

	Non-metric			**Metric**
weight (UK)			1 ounce (oz)	= 28.35 grams (g)
	16 ounces	=	1 pound (lb)	= 0.454 kilogram (kg)
	14 pounds	=	1 stone (st)	= 6.356 kilograms
	8 stone	=	1 hundredweight (cwt)	= 50.8 kilograms
	20 cwt	=	1 (long) ton	= 1,016.04 kilograms
			1 tonne (t)	= 1,000 kilograms
weight (US)			1 ounce (oz)	= 28.35 grams (g)
	16 ounces	=	1 pound (lb)	= 0.454 kilogram (kg)
	100 pounds	=	1 hundredweight (cwt)	= 45.359 kilograms
	20 cwt	=	1 (short) ton (t)	= 907.18 kilograms
length			1 inch (1 in; 11 1)	= 25.4 millimetres (mm)
	12 inches	=	1 foot (1 ft; 11)	= 30.48 centimetres (cm)
	3 feet	=	1 yard (yd)	= 0.914 metre (m)
	1760 yards	=	1 mile (m)	= 1.609 kilometres (km)
surface			1 square inch (sq in)	= 6.452 sq centimetres (cm²)
	144 sq inches	=	1 sq foot (sq ft)	= 929.03 cm²
	9 sq feet	=	1 sq yard (sq yd)	= 0.836 sq metre (m²)
	4,840 sq yards	=	1 acre	= 0.405 hectare (ha)
	640 acres	=	1 sq mile (sq m)	= 2.59 km²
volume			1 cubic inch (cu in)	= 16.4 cm³ or cc
	1728 cubic inches	=	1 cubic foot (cu ft)	= 0.028 m³
	27 cubic feet	=	1 cubic yard (cu yd)	= 0.765 m³
capacity (UK)	20 fluid ounces (fl oz)	=	1 pint (pt)	= 0.568 litre (l)
	2 pints	=	1 quart (qt)	= 1.136 litres
	4 quarts	=	1 gallon (gal)	= 4.546 litres
capacity (US)	16 fluid ounces (fl oz)	=	1 pint (pt)	= 0.473 liter (l)
	2 pints	=	1 quart (qt)	= 0.946 liter
	4 quarts	=	1 gallon (gal)	= 3.785 liters